Be Visible Or Vanish

T0382968

The world of the academic researcher is changing; it used to be enough to work hard, do your research and get your results published. Not so these days. Universities now expect researchers to share their work with the world, as widely as possible. 'Publish or perish' has been replaced by a new mantra, and the pressure is on.

In this insightful book, Inger Mewburn and Simon Clews look at some of the most common presentation scenarios that researchers will face when talking about their work. Starting in academia with the deceptively simple art of writing a good email and working through lectures, conference presentations and lightning talks, the book then moves 'off campus' and explores talking to the media, making elevator pitches and creating an effective digital presence on social media.

Offering detailed looks at 19 different presentation formats, Mewburn and Clews tap into their vast experience in the field to analyse the challenges and opportunities aligned with each case study and to map out the route to success. With a lightness of touch and an often humorous approach, *Be Visible Or Vanish: Engage, Influence and Ensure Your Research Has Impact* will show you what it takes to achieve that holy grail of modern academia... impact.

This text will be invaluable for students, academics and researchers hoping to effectively communicate complex information in a way that can be understood and appreciated by their peers, colleagues and the wider world.

Inger Mewburn, known throughout the academic world as *The Thesis Whisperer*, is the Director of Researcher Development at the Australian National University. Her blog is considered the 'go to' place for all things PhD-related and her hugely successful podcasts have taken those insights into a whole new dimension. Visit: https://thesiswhisperer.com/

Simon Clews, the inaugural Director of the Melbourne Engagement Lab at Melbourne University and Australia's most experienced literary events creator, works with writers and academics around the world to help them improve their written and oral communication and develop their careers as effective communicators and providers of creative, well-written non-fiction for non-academic audiences. Visit: www.simonclews.com

Insider Guides to Success in Academia

Series Editors:

Helen Kara,

Independent Researcher, UK and

Pat Thomson,

The University of Nottingham, UK.

The *Insiders' Guides to Success in Academia* address topics too small for a full-length book on their own, but too big to cover in a single chapter or article. These topics have often been the stuff of discussions on social media, or of questions in our workshops. We designed this series to answer these questions in to provide practical support for doctoral and early career researchers. It is geared to concerns that many people experience. Readers will find these books to be companions who provide advice and help to make sense of everyday life in the contemporary university.

We have therefore:

(1) invited scholars with deep and specific expertise to write. Our writers use their research and professional experience to provide well-grounded strategies to particular situations.

(2) asked writers to collaborate. Most of the books are produced by writers who live in different countries, or work in different disciplines, or both. While it is difficult for any book to cover all the diverse contexts in which potential readers live and work, the different perspectives and contexts of writers goes some way to address this problem.

We understand that the use of the term 'academia' might be read as meaning the university, but we take a broader view.

Pat does indeed work in a university, but spent a long time working outside of one. Helen is an independent researcher and sometimes works with universities. Both of us understand academic – or scholarly – work as now being conducted in a range of sites, from museums and the public sector to industry research and development laboratories. Academic work is also often undertaken by networks which bring together scholars in various locations. All of our writers understand that this is the case, and use the term 'academic' in this wider sense.

These books are pocket sized so that they can be carried around and visited again and again. Most of the books have a mix of examples, stories and exercises as well as explanation and advice. They are written in a collegial tone, and from a position of care as well as knowledge.

Together with our writers, we hope that each book in the series can make a positive contribution to the work and life of readers, so that you too can become insiders in scholarship.

Helen Kara, PhD FAcSS
Independent researcher
https://helenkara.com/
@DrHelenKara (Twitter/Insta)
Pat Thomson PhD PSM FAcSS FRSA
Professor of Education, The University of Nottingham
https://patthomson.net
@ThomsonPat

Books in the Series:

Your PhD Survival Guide
Planning, Writing and Succeeding in Your Final Year
Katherine Firth, Liam Connell, and Peta Freestone

Making Sense of Academic Conferences
Presenting, Participating and Organising
James Burford and Emily F. Henderson

Be Visible Or Vanish

Engage, Influence and Ensure Your Research Has Impact

Inger Mewburn
and Simon Clews

Routledge
Taylor & Francis Group

LONDON AND NEW YORK

Designed cover image: © Getty Images

First published 2023
by Routledge
4 Park Square, Milton Park, Abingdon, Oxon OX14 4RN

and by Routledge
605 Third Avenue, New York, NY 10158

Routledge is an imprint of the Taylor & Francis Group, an informa business

British Library Cataloguing-in-Publication Data
A catalogue record for this book is available from the British Library

Library of Congress Cataloging-in-Publication Data
Names: Mewburn, Inger, author. | Clews, Simon, author.
Title: Be visible or vanish: engage, influence and ensure your research
has impact / Inger Mewburn, Simon Clews.
Description: Abingdon, Oxon; New York, NY: Routledge, 2023. |
Series: Insider guides to success in academia |
Includes bibliographical references and index. |
Identifiers: LCCN 2022042232 (print) | LCCN 2022042233 (ebook) |
ISBN 9781032049946 (hardback) | ISBN 9781032054803 (paperback) |
ISBN 9781003197713 (ebook)
Subjects: LCSH: Communication in higher education. |
College teachers—Professional relationships. | Lectures and lecturing. |
Scholarly publishing. | Research. Classification: LCC LB1778.M48 2023 (print) |
LCC LB1778 (ebook) | DDC 378.1/2—dc23/eng/20221025
LC record available at https://lccn.loc.gov/2022042232
LC ebook record available at https://lccn.loc.gov/2022042233

ISBN: 9781032049946 (hbk)
ISBN: 9781032054803 (pbk)
ISBN: 9781003197713 (ebk)

DOI: 10.4324/9781003197713

Typeset in Bembo
by codeMantra

Contents

Acknowledgements

We'd like to express our sincere gratitude to and admiration for Emma Driver, editor extraordinaire, who came on board right before the end to whip us into shape. Emma was introduced to both of us by NewSouth Publishing and is now the first person we call when we need to make a bunch of words into an actual book. Thanks Emma! And thanks should also go to the inimitable John Lamp who originally challenged researchers to "get visible or vanish".

Inger

I would like to thank my beautiful husband Luke for quietly placing coffee cups at my elbow at strategic intervals and for being OK with me disappearing for most of January 2022 to finish this book. As a reward for enduring seven books in eight years, I promise not to write one in 2023. I'd also like to thank the Omicron variant for forcing everyone else into a 'shadow lockdown' so I didn't feel like I was particularly missing out on anything. Shout out to my son Brendan for being a good office mate and for saying 'I believe in you' or 'You can finish this' or 'You say this every time' whenever I said I hated writing.

Simon

Everyone who knows me is aware of my dislike for acknowledgements; my preference is always for the personal, private thank you over the public one. So, to those who support and/or put up with me – you know who you are – thank you as always. But, as a lazy, slack, deadline-avoiding writer, I do owe a huge debt to my co-author. If it wasn't for her encouragement, praise, motivation, threats and general guilt-tripping, you'd only have a half a book in your hands. Of course, it would be the better half, but you'd probably be feeling a bit short-changed on the purchase price. So, in the inimitable words of *The Thesis Whisperer:* thank you, colleague.

Introduction

Academia is now a highly competitive profession. Researchers increasingly need to demonstrate the 'impact' of their research and share it with a wide range of audiences. The old rule of 'publish or perish' is being replaced by the need to 'be visible or vanish'.

There are many books on presenting research, including books written specifically for students presenting in academic settings. These books offer useful advice, but they often leave out crucial context. Different types of presentations have different rules for success. You need to explain your research to a journalist in a different way to how you would explain it to a colleague you meet at a conference. What you say to a stray billionaire in a lift will be different to what you say to the dean of your school when you are asking for a new piece of equipment, and different again to what you say about your research during a job interview. You will need to talk about your research in the tea room, during team meetings, on email, via social media and in the corridors at conferences. These highly varied scenarios call for different types of communication skills.

The book outlines 16 different types of research presentation types you might encounter as an academic researcher. Starting in the classroom and tea rooms and campus, then broadening to the outside world, we'll tell you how to prepare for each type of presentation and what makes a presentation not just competent but good. It's important to consider the purpose of the communication, and who is listening, so you can adjust your speaking style and content. Each type of presentation has an audience of some sort, and different audiences have different expectations. These expectations are strong, and breaking them can lead to discomfort for your audience, and maybe even a poor reception. For instance, if you turn up to an academic conference and recite an epic poem instead of giving a walkthrough of your research, you have powerfully broken audience expectations. They will be unsure how to react – should they clap at the end like they would in a coffee house poetry slam night? How do you ask questions about a poem? In situations like this, you are more likely to end to an awkward silence than praise.

It's good to bend the rules: it makes you memorable. But while challenging the audience is one thing, being illegible is another. Breaking the rules so hard that your presentation is unrecognisable as a research presentation carries risks. This book will give you confidence to break rules knowingly. It will show you how to shine when you find yourself on stage for a festival panel, or unexpectedly face to face with a world-famous academic in front of your conference poster.

We wrote this book because research educators like us understand that presenting research is a huge challenge for beginners and experts alike. Both of us have made a living for decades teaching researchers how to communicate well. We're both in demand as teachers because communicating well is hard! Our human brains are good at remembering and understanding stories but less good at comprehending and recalling facts and figures. We can all struggle to understand complicated, abstract concepts. Human brains like concreteness: things we can see, hear, smell, touch and taste, and stories that have recognisable beginnings, middles and ends. To be a good communicator you need to be able to create strong through-lines for your research stories, and apply clever analogies and metaphors to help you explain abstract concepts. In this book, we share everything we have learned over decades of helping researchers communicate to influence and impress.

We've organised this book around the real-world communication challenges you will face as an early-career researcher and beyond. The book is divided into four main parts, each of which tackles different kinds of presentation scenarios. Part I deals with presentations that happen inside our university walls as part of both academic work and study. We'll cover things like milestone presentations, research meetings and teaching interacting in academic tea rooms. In Part II, we discuss presentations that happen inside universities but are aimed at creating research impact. This section includes situations like lightening talks and competitions like the Three Minute Thesis. In Part III, we tackle presentation scenarios that are completely outside the academy like talking to the media, sharing on social media and being on panels at festivals. In Part IV, we offer advice that applies to every presentation type and setting: speaking to camera, controlling your visuals, calmly answering questions from the audience and dealing with intellectual property.

The book is designed to be read from start to finish, or for you to jump straight to the chapter devoted to your immediate needs. Within the first three parts of the book, we have short chapters dealing with different presentation types. Each chapter has a summary at the top called 'TL;DR' (too long; didn't read!). We then include a short 'In a nutshell' section, which describes the type of presentation the chapter deals with. We go on to give advice on how to prepare, and then some 'masterclass' tips to elevate your performance from competent to amazing. Each chapter includes a final section called 'Notes on remote mode' to help you translate these ideas when you can't be there in person and some recommended reading to explore the ideas further.

As we write this book, in Australia, the COVID-19 pandemic rages on and may well do so for some time. Over the last two years, many of us have spent weeks or months working from our homes. But being trapped inside doesn't mean that the job of being an academic is any less public. Conferences have moved online, TV interviews are staged in kitchens and bedrooms, and we all have become familiar with 'Zoom fatigue' after days of seemingly endless online meetings. While the roots of this book are formed in the face-to-face world, these same presentation scenarios exist online, now often alongside the three-dimensional world in the dreaded 'blended mode', where some of us are on screens and the rest are in person. The tea room has become a Twitter stream, and the Three Minute Thesis is now a video instead of a stage performance. While many of the 'rules' for success remain unchanged, applying the principles of good performance to fully online and blended spaces is complex. To reflect this new reality, the 'Notes on remote mode' sections have advice for translating our tips for a great performance into online mode(s). We expect these modes to be enduring and our future lives to be a blend of face-to-face and remote modes. This book will help you be comfortable in both spaces.

Who are we?

We are experienced researcher developers who teach people how to communicate their research to a range of audiences and for different purposes. We have been teaching PhD students, postdocs and working academics how to present their research for a collective 40 years.

For 15 years, Simon was the Director of the Melbourne Engagement Lab at Melbourne University, where he trained, facilitated, motivated and occasionally inspired academic researchers to share their discoveries with the outside world. These days he continues his love of 'being in the same room as really, really smart people' as an in-demand written and oral communications expert working with researchers and writers around the world.

Inger is the creator and editor of the world-famous *The Thesis Whisperer* blog and has been working with PhD students, postdocs and academics since 2006. She has held the role of director of researcher development at the Australian National University (ANU) for the last ten years, where her teaching practice centres on writing and communications. Inger is also a working researcher who publishes papers and book chapters and even commercialises her research. In addition to persuading colleagues of the validity of the products her team makes from their research, and telling journalists about it, she's had to learn to pitch for money from investors and sell a product to clients.

This book is a compendium of everything we have been teaching in our respective classrooms – we've enjoyed writing it together and are excited to share what we know about successful academic presentations with you.

Part I

Classrooms and colleagues

Aspiring novelists are told to 'write what you know', so we are starting this book with lessons learned from spending many years inside the academy. We are old hands at working the classroom and navigating the power structures of academia – one of us even made it all the way to professor (while the other was much more sensible and stayed in roles that were much more fun!).

Between us we've taught thousands of early, mid and even late career researchers how to conduct themselves on stage, but we've spent almost the same amount of time mentoring people and helping them solve interpersonal problems that happen when you fail to communicate well. In all these years we've come to know one thing: your biggest career asset is your brain and your ability to do research. BUT: unless you can talk to people about that research, in different settings and for different purposes, you won't leverage the benefits of that big, beautiful brain.

In this section of the book, we take you from elaborate, ritualised academic settings like the PhD viva to 'off-the-cuff' talks with colleagues, where you have to think on your feet. This stuff is the bread and butter of academic life, so pull your seat up to the table and get stuck in!

DOI: 10.4324/9781003197713-1

1 Assessment and exam presentations

TL;DR

- Know your material. It's important to be calm and confident in assessment presentations, otherwise people will start actively looking for mistakes and problems.
- Focus on method as much as findings. Your peers and advisors will be looking to critique the way you did something as much as what you found.
- Know your literature selection strategy. It's now impossible to read everything. Have a rationale so you can fend off 'Why haven't you read ...' questions.
- Remember: your ability to answer questions is being tested. Try to anticipate possible questions and draft answers in advance of the presentation.

In a nutshell

Up until the early 2000s, people just went ahead and did a PhD for years and years. Under the influence of 'neoliberal discourses of efficiency' (that's academic-speak for running a university like a business), universities now want to get rid of people who hang around too long. Universities use milestones

DOI: 10.4324/9781003197713-2

to monitor progress and manage student load. A milestone is a written record in the system, usually prepared by your supervisor, commenting on your academic progress.

From your point of view, milestones usually take the form of written reports accompanied by a presentation about work in progress. Milestone systems vary, so you may not always have to do a presentation, but it's common enough that you should always be prepared. These are high-stakes moments in candidature. It's vital you perform well in milestone presentations, or you can be literally put 'at risk' and 'managed out'.

It's rare to be given a grade for your milestone – it tends to be a pass/fail kind of situation – but supervisors will be asked to comment on performance. The quality of your performance will affect whether you are allowed to continue in your program and can sometimes be used to attract collaboration and extra resources. In our experience, supervisors often underplay the importance of milestone presentations, so don't be fooled. In disputes with supervisors, it's common for milestone records of poor performance to be pulled out as evidence and used against you.

The idea of the milestone presentation is twofold: to see if you are on track to complete, and to allow regular peer review and feedback from outside your supervisory team. While you can sometimes to be asked to do a 'table read' of a talk to a small panel, milestone presentations are more likely to be a public performance. The audience may contain your supervisor team, the faculty, peers and other invited experts. In some systems, a conference presentation may be counted towards a mid-candidature milestone obligation.

Sometimes universities set aside a special day and ask candidates to present in a conference-style format, with tea breaks between paper sessions. This format is challenging as it is far more likely that you will have a big audience of other students and a broad range of faculty who will ask a broad range of questions. Other universities handle it at a local level and have a day set aside once a week or once a month for research presentations, usually as part of a regular seminar series. In this case, the audience is usually limited to immediate department members and the range of questions is probably narrower.

Sometimes universities leave the arrangements up to the supervision panel and the candidate, who invite the audience they specifically want to vet the research. If the audience is open, remember: milestone presentations are a form of academic theatre. Expect some people to show up purely to witness (or contribute to) the drama!

How to prepare

As with all presentations, think audience first. Whatever format applies to you, the audience is likely to be composed of the following sorts of people:

- Your supervisor team
- Fellow PhD students and (possibly) interested masters and honours students
- Other faculty members.

Each of these audiences has slightly different expectations.

Your team of supervisors will often be asked to write a short assessment of your performance, so they will be watching you carefully. We have seen some supervisors act atrociously towards their candidates at milestone presentations, publicly taking them to task for perceived deficiencies. We think this is a sackable offence, but at the same time we caution you: *do not expect your supervisor to defend you against attacks.* Part of becoming an independent researcher is to learn to defend your work, and many supervisors believe the best way to learn this is by doing it.

The role of the supervisor in a milestone presentation is to be supportively critical. By this, we mean that supervisors may publicly acknowledge weaknesses in your work when it is criticised by others. Try to take supervisor comments in the spirit they are probably meant: to help you to understand the feedback. We've seen students get really hurt by supervisor comments that they feel (understandably) should have been said in private beforehand. Sometimes this is true, but supervisors are not super geniuses and can get too close to the work, making it hard for them to see the problems until their peers point them out.

We divide the student audience into three general types: your friends, your friendly competitors and show-offs. Most of your fellow students are interested in measuring their own research progress against yours and learning from your experience. Friends are easy – stack the audience with as many as you are allowed. Ask your friends to take notes for you, especially about the questions that are asked during the session. Multiple notes from friendly people, with different points of view, can be remarkably helpful in sharpening your messages. Then there are a few students who, in our experience, use other students' milestones as an opportunity to show off their own expertise and assert dominance. This sort of student likes to ask clever questions but, because they are inexperienced, the questions can be difficult to interpret and answer. Check out our section on answering questions and dealing with trolls at the end of the book.

Finally, to the faculty. The role of the faculty is to uphold standards in their department and help ensure that the research being presented is doable within a standard PhD timeline. We divide these further into two main types: generous and interested souls, and members of 'the peanut gallery'. The peanut gallery is a term from American vaudeville of the late 1800s, used to describe rowdy patrons who would throw their peanut shells at a performer, presumably for kicks. Think about trolls on social media – same urge.

Really experienced faculty members, even the interested and generous souls, can and will ask devastatingly simple and difficult-to-answer questions. For example, Inger's favourite question in a confirmation presentation is 'How long do you think it will take to complete these interviews and analyse the data?' Inger has a rough metric of six hours of analysis per hour of interview and will do a quick 'back-of-the-envelope' calculation to see if the candidate has set aside enough time. Make sure you talk to your supervisor about their own pet questions, and be prepared to answer disarmingly simple queries about your processes and techniques.

Most faculty members, in our experience, fall into the generous and interested category: they remember what doing a PhD was like and are there to help. The members of the peanut gallery, on the other hand, can take their mission to 'uphold standards' way too seriously. These people subscribe to the 'sink or swim' school of PhD pedagogy and think subjecting candidates to trial by fire is the best way to ensure quality (it isn't).

As you can see, the milestone presentation is an interesting challenge. There will be people there with strong opinions about your research and, depending on the research culture in your faculty, they might be unhelpful in the way they present these opinions.

How to be good at it

The milestone presentations you give at the beginning, middle and end of your PhD will be different in tone and flavour. To that end, we have separated our advice into four sections: the first presentation, the mid-candidature presentation, the pre-submission seminar and the oral examination (viva voce).

First presentation ('confirmation')

In most PhD programs, the first milestone is called the confirmation, which is suggestive of academia's roots in the church. The PhD confirmation is usually the end of your probation period and a chance to get more eyes on your proposed research to ensure that it is both doable and worth doing. Some universities make further funding contingent on passing or will not allow people to put in an ethics application until this milestone is met.

Usually, you'll be asked to submit a fully worked-up research proposal and one completed chapter, and present on both of these to the faculty and supervision panel.

Universities vary on how seriously they take this first milestone. Inger went to Melbourne University, who took it very seriously: people could fail – and did. Failing meant repeating the presentation three months later. Some people were unable to complete this hurdle after a second attempt and were redirected into a master's degree program, or asked to leave. At the Australian National University (ANU), where she works now, there is no process to make a person repeat a milestone … yet! As universities experience funding pressures, these funnel through to systems like milestones, which can be an efficient way to 'shed student load'. Our point is this: even if your university has a laissez-faire approach right now, there is no guarantee it will stay that way. Treat the confirmation very seriously.

You will usually be given between 20 and 40 minutes for your confirmation presentation. The key challenge here is to present a lot of detail in an engaging way. Sometimes the best way to tell you what to do is to tell you what *not* to do:

- **Don't assume your audience has enough background to grasp the importance and originality of your research.** Your research, by definition, is original. Presenting enough – and the right kind – of background to enable people to understand your research and its contribution makes the confirmation presentation uniquely difficult. You need to find the balance: skimming over 'what everyone knows' and providing the more esoteric 'need to knows' specific to this particular piece of research. We suggest that supervisors are not always the best people to ask if you've achieved the right balance. Try the material out on a peer who is in the same field or another faculty member.

- **Don't look like you already know the answers to the research questions you are asking**. The idea of a confirmation proposal is to show people that you have set up an investigation properly. Share preliminary findings, if you have them, but be careful how you frame them. Being too certain of the answers early in the process is the best way to invite a hail of shells from the peanut gallery.

- **Don't underestimate the time your tasks will take**. Most experienced researchers will have done a similar project to yours and will know how long things take to do – things like bench work or interviews. An experienced researcher will know that 100 one-hour structured interviews could easily take you up to 600 hours or more to process. If you don't have four months allowed in your plan to do this work, you will look underprepared. Identify and think through all the basic time constraints of the project and use a tool like the Program Evaluation and Review Technique (PERT) to estimate the time on task – then scale up appropriately.[1]

- **Don't overclaim the originality of the work**. A sure sign of a newbie is someone who says 'There is no research on …'. There is just so much literature out there – it's hardly ever true that no one has been there before. Use hedging language, like 'To my knowledge, although there has been research on X, Y has received less attention'.

- **Don't be all literature, no action**. While it's important to prove that you've read enough to identify the gap/opportunity for new research, don't forget that the audience needs to know *how* you intend to do the research.
- **Don't give the impression that you have everything covered**. Be a bit humble. An academic audience can read confidence, especially in the early stages of a project, as arrogance. This advice is especially pertinent for people coming back to study after a stint in the workplace. In the workplace, it's important to show competence and asking for help can be read as a weakness. By contrast, students are expected to ask for help, especially early on in their research. Even if you feel very confident, showing some 'strategic vulnerability' will encourage people to offer help, rather than trying to find each crack in your armour. One simple way to seek help is to put a couple of questions you need answers for in your presentation slide deck at the end. People tend to focus on the start or end of a presentation, and a few thoughtful questions can direct the energy of the room into areas where you can really use help.
- Mid-candidature presentation

Mid-candidature reviews often have lower stakes than the confirmation or oral exam, so our best advice is to try to enjoy the opportunity to get some feedback on your work. The easiest way to approach this kind of presentation is to think about it like a slightly expanded conference paper. Although you will have to give the audience some overview of the project and where you are up to, you still need to tell a story. We suggest a 'spotlight' approach: a short background section to situate the study, followed by a deep dive on one experiment, chapter or theoretical argument.

We suggest the spotlight approach because research can be a big old mess in the middle of a project. There might have been major changes you need to account for – even a whole change of topic. Putting together one of these presentations can feel a bit like tidying only the public areas of your house for visitors. If you feel like you haven't really got it together, don't worry too much: almost everyone feels this way. Preparing a mid-candidature presentation is a good way to clean up and take stock – and to contemplate the horizon. Seize the day. Trying to make it all make sense for other people can sometimes help it make sense for you, even if clarity is an illusion right now.

Speaking of illusions, everyone knows your projections of the future of the research and the completion date are probably fictitious, but don't forget to include a Gantt chart or diagram that shows how long it might take to finish the project. Seeing a concrete plan gives your supervisor team a sense of security and signals to the audience that you are a professional researcher who knows how to manage a project.

Pre-submission seminar

Most universities have a requirement for the candidate to present an overview of the thesis three to six months out from submission. This presentation is the last chance for feedback from your peers and for the faculty to try to assess the quality of the work. While this presentation can feel high stakes, it's often not as big a deal as you imagine. The mood in the room is often more celebratory than critical. Although the peanut gallery can turn up to this event, they are usually more subdued.

The biggest challenge in this presentation will be showing the whole thesis without drowning in detail. You will only have time for an overview of the work done, not a deep dive into everything. One way to approach it is to think about the findings of Gerry Mullins and Margaret Kiley, who interviewed thesis examiners about what a 'good' thesis looks like. They came up with a useful list, which also works as a good checklist for this presentation. Think about how you can convince the audience that your thesis will:

- Be a report of work that others would want to read
- Tell a compelling story articulately while pre-empting inevitable critiques
- Be able to carry the reader into complex realms while informing and educating them
- Be sufficiently speculative or original to suggest you would be an interesting future colleague.[2]

Oral examination (viva voce)

There have been whole books written, and many tearful stories told, about the oral exam or 'viva'.

The viva experience varies from university to university – even from student to student. Some people are given a chance to do a presentation at the start and are asked useful questions; others are put in front of a whiteboard with a pen and grilled. There is just not sufficient room here to capture the complexity of what you might face, but the advice to think 'audience first' still holds.

The viva audience is unique – they are the first people you are presenting to who have actually read your whole dissertation. This is the first time you don't have to worry about drowning someone in detail – you've already done that! The challenge for you in this situation is to convince them that you wrote every line – and that you know why you made decisions during the research process.

On his Viva Survivors website, Nathan Ryder suggests a 'Why-How-What' structure for your viva.[3] Start with why you did the research, specifically the contribution to knowledge you wanted to make. Briefly talk about the methods you used to carry out the study; you might want to include any diversions or abandoned avenues of investigation that help your panel understand your decision-making process. Finally, outline the key findings and their implications. You might want to finish with a 'What now?' section where you talk about what other work remains to be done or could follow on – and, possibly, your own plans.

The heart of the viva is the questioning. It can be helpful to prepare a list of answers to possible questions as a way of 'studying' your own document and making sure you know everything that is in there. The following list is adapted from a paper by Vernon Trafford and Shosh Leshem.[4] Not all of them will be relevant, but try writing 200–300 words on the ten most relevant ones and then tackle others if you have time:

- Why did you choose this topic for your doctoral study?
- How did you arrive at your conceptual framework and/or theoretical components of your study?
- How did you use your conceptual/theoretical framework to design your research and analyse your findings?
- How did you arrive at your research design?
- What other forms of research did you consider?
- How would you justify your choice of methodology?
- Please explain your methodology to us.
- Why did you choose to use those methods of data collection?
- What other methods of data collection did you consider and why were they rejected?
- Were you disappointed with your conclusions?
- How do your conclusions relate to your conceptual framework?

- How generalisable are your findings – and why?
- What is your contribution to knowledge?
- How important are your findings and to whom?
- What are the strengths and weaknesses of your research?
- What would you do differently if you repeated your research?
- What are you going to do after you gain your doctorate?
- How is gaining your doctorate going to help your career?
- What are you going to publish from your thesis?

As you write the answers to your questions, make a note of which pages in your thesis are most relevant in case you need to flip through the document during the exam. If you are using a printout in the presentation, use Post-it notes to make your document easier to navigate in a hurry. It also sounds really impressive if you can say 'As I said on page 124 …'.

Finally – and we know this is much easier said than done – try to stay calm. As Inger's therapist is fond of saying, 'calm is control'. If a plane is crashing, the person panicking will not be the one who successfully finds and uses the exit. Do your preparation and trust that it will serve you well.

Notes on remote mode

- Selecting examiners for a PhD can be difficult, so it's highly likely that at least one person will have to beam into a viva: in remote jurisdictions, like New Zealand and Australia, it's common for the viva to be conducted entirely online.
- The jury is out on whether doing your viva remotely is more nerve-racking than in person. You can pick up a lot about how a person is responding to information by minute variations in their expressions and posture as they listen; many people will also make noises like sighs. In face-to-face

settings, it's relatively easy to pick up these cues and adjust your delivery, but in remote mode there is less information available to you via a small picture on the screen – especially if the person is on mute. We don't have any great advice to overcome these limitations. Without these cues, you can only fall back on what you know about the person already. We strongly suggest that you read papers and articles the examiners have written before going into the exam, and, if at all possible, talk to someone who knows the person and has worked with them before. This can help you 'profile' the people on the other side of the table so you can anticipate behaviour. If you know their research interests and concerns, you will know what areas of your work may be controversial; you will also get an idea of their preferred styles of communication and adjust as much as is practicable.

- The advantage of the online format is they can see less of you too, so if you are nervous, you won't be showing it as much as you think you are!
- 'Calm is control' also applies to preparation. Check you are familiar with the technology you will be using and have a backup plan for getting in touch with the chair (perhaps by phone) so you can troubleshoot any problems.
- Dress as you would in person, so you feel more professional – whatever that means for you. It can help to stick a picture of someone you love on the edge of you monitor so that you have a friendly face in the 'audience'.
- Finally, no one knows if you have the cat on your lap during a Zoom exam. Go for it!

Further reading

There are a lot of excellent books in the How To Do a PhD genre, many of which include at least a small section on oral examinations. There are few books that deal with assessment presentations as a separate topic, but a couple that cover preparing for the final viva, for example 'The PhD Viva: how to prepare for your oral examination' by Peter Smith.[5] A particular favourite of ours is a self-published book called *Fail Your Viva – Twelve Steps To Failing Your PhD (And Fifty-Eight Tips For Passing)* by Nathan Ryder. Nathan teaches workshops on the Viva all over the UK and has a number of good publications and pamphlets available on his website: http://www.nathanryder.co.uk/ebooks/.

Notes

1   Daniel D. Roman, 'The PERT system: An appraisal of program evaluation review technique', *Journal of the Academy of Management* 5, no. 1 (1962): 57–65, https://www.jstor.org/stable/254602.

2   Gerry Mullins and Margaret Kiley, '"It's a PhD, not a Nobel Prize": How experienced examiners assess research theses', *Studies in Higher Education* 27, no. 4 (2002): 369–86, https://doi.org/10.1080/0307507022000011507.

3   Nathan Ryder, '7 tips for a viva presentation', Viva Survivors, 27 September 2019, http://viva-survivors.com/2019/09/7-tips-for-a-viva-presentation/.

4   Vernon Trafford and Shosh Leshem, 'Starting at the end to undertake doctoral research: Predictable questions as stepping stones', *Higher Education Review* 34, no. 1 (2002): 31–49, https://www.researchgate.net/publication/310055048.

5   Smith, Peter, *The PhD viva: How to prepare for oral examination*, Bloomsbury, 2014.

2 Research group meetings

TL;DR

- Build trust through professional courtesy. Turn up to your meetings on time, have the right materials with you and always seek to be helpful.
- Bring new findings and report problems – especially problems that others might be able to solve. Make it a safe space for failure and struggle by offering helpful critique to others instead of shaming and blaming.
- Collaborate to make the meeting efficient by knowing when to stop detailed explanations and call a separate meeting to discuss further.
- Be careful how you comment on others' work, especially if you are new. Make sure you understand the 'why' of someone's research before telling them they should do it another way.

In a nutshell

Not all researchers have team meetings. Regular meetings are more common in the sciences where research work can be portioned out in smaller parcels that contribute to a larger

DOI: 10.4324/9781003197713-3

whole. Meetings to share work in progress help co-ordinate the work of the whole lab towards collective goals. Many labs have weekly meetings, but sometimes meetings are more frequent, even daily, depending on the nature of the work being done. Disciplines outside science don't tend to collaborate as much, so research meetings will be less frequent. In these disciplines, you may never have research meetings; if you do, they are more likely to be brainstorming or coordinating work to meet milestones, and less about sharing details of the work in progress.

Research meetings are a chance to leverage the 'hive mind' and develop collective research capacity. Gathering a diverse group of people with different levels of experience and expertise together is a great way to solve problems. Group meetings are particularly powerful when participants are people at various stages of their careers. You might be lucky to find yourself in a group comprising research assistants, PhD students, postdocs and professors. From the early-career researcher point of view, these kinds of lab meetings also offer an opportunity for what Jean Lave and Etienne Wenger called 'legitimate peripheral participation': a chance to eavesdrop on what others are doing and learn from their achievements – and mistakes.[1]

Whatever the format and frequency, research meetings are critical to generating robust research outcomes. They are also – and we cannot stress this enough – critical to your future career as a researcher.

Research meetings are also an opportunity to demonstrate your own professional competence and build trusted bonds with others. Academia is a truly international, mobile profession so people move on, but they carry their 'social knowledge' of you with them. Positive social knowledge is more likely to lead to word-of-mouth recommendations for future work. We can't stress enough how important personal recommendations are in the academic job market – and outside it, for that matter. There is nothing like working together on common aims to build social trust. Social trust leads to glowing references and early knowledge of further opportunities. For career reasons alone, research group meetings should be one of the most important things in your diary.

How to prepare

Research meetings have various degrees of structure. A highly structured meeting will have an agenda, speaker order and time limits. A lightly structured meeting might start with a set of problems that need attention or just a round-table 'report in' from each member. Your key responsibility in a research meeting is to share your knowledge and listen to other people carefully. This is a lot harder than it sounds, so read on!

You need to signal 'progress' to the rest of the meeting participants. Your progress may be slow – that's usually OK. If you don't have findings, bring something else to the table. Here's a (non-exhaustive) list of materials you might want to bring to a meeting:

- Findings and/or preliminary analysis
- Descriptions of problems encountered
- A description of an experimental set-up or interview protocol, etc.
- A list of papers you're planning to read and/or a digest of what you found out through reading
- Ideas for future work
- A timetable of planned activities
- A publication you are planning or have just published.

Remember that you are there to listen more than talk most of the time. Here's a (non-exhaustive) list of things you can learn if you ask the right questions and let people talk:

- How to publish strategically – what journals and outlets are most respected and how to navigate the peer-review process
- How to find literature, decide what is relevant or not and stay in touch with new literature
- How to manage your data, including lab books and bibliography
- In some cases, how to do a bad job so you know what *not* to do!

Some meetings will include short presentations to others, with or without slides. These are (hopefully) low-stakes presentations, among trusted collaborators, but it doesn't mean that the basic principle of 'audience first' is not relevant. Watch what other people do and copy the practices of the person who seems to get the most respect from the team: they are probably doing something right.

If you are presenting findings or ideas, make sure to include your key assumptions, motivations and relevant background to help people understand what is happening. Everyone is busy, and some will need a bit of history of the work, or of the thinking, before they can understand what is going on right now. Don't be upset if people don't remember what you were doing: academia is a busy place. This is a learning opportunity, helping you to sharpen your ability to answer questions and explain complicated concepts and ideas to others.

Spend a bit of time thinking about physical constraints you are dealing with. How are the furniture and AV arranged in the room? Will everyone be able to hear and see the same things? A bit of forward thinking will help you to decide if you need to use the projector or make some handouts – or perhaps both.

We think presentation aids are just as useful in meetings as they are when you are on the stage. A graph, table or diagram on the screen can help focus attention and give people a more information-rich package to react to. Preparing these materials can also help you think through what you want to say.

Don't forget that a paper handout can serve the same function of focusing attention, especially if there is no AV equipment. Handouts have the advantage of being durable copies that people can mark up and give you feedback on: a table or figure can more easily be corrected with a pen than on a projection. Inger makes paper handouts for café meetings, where it tends to be noisy, or when there is a group of people who don't know each other well. Some people will prefer to write notes on your handouts and give these to you later, rather than speaking up in front of a big group.

How to be good at it

Sometimes meeting cultures are set up and resistant to change. You may find yourself in a situation where the team meeting culture is dysfunctional. As Inger is fond of saying, 'The fish rots from the head down'. Poor meeting culture is usually the fault of poor leadership. Sometimes all it takes is for people to speak up and point out the problem for things to change, but be careful about speaking out if you are a newcomer. Take your time to understand why the situation exists so that you can approach the problem diplomatically.

Try to be mindful of the time constraints and the needs of others. You don't win friends and allies by always 'sucking all the air out of the room' with your own problems and concerns. Be mindful of how much time you are taking up – research shows that some people will be listened to more than others because of their race or gender. Older white men take note: it will often be assumed you are the top of the hierarchy because of the body you occupy. If you occupy a position of privilege, remember to 'make space' for others. This means self-monitoring and remembering to invite others to speak.

It can be hard to avoid being a time hog if the discussion becomes intense and detailed – these conversations can derail a whole meeting agenda. It can be a good idea to take highly specialised questions on notice: the best time to address these might be in a smaller forum.

If you're in charge of organising meetings, here are a few tips.

- If you have a lot of busy people, organise the meetings far in advance. Busy people will find it easier to arrange their diary around regular standing meetings than *ad hoc* arrangements.
- Consider timing carefully. Lunch meetings can be surprisingly convivial if they are only once a week, but it's unreasonable to ask people to give up their lunchtime every day. Late on Friday may roll neatly into lab drinks but will not necessarily be the best time for people to focus, and may exclude carers.
- Consider people with caring duties: for example, early mornings or late afternoons can interfere with school drop-off and pickup; people caring for relatives with disabilities can have a lot of appointments to attend and will appreciate early notice and flexible meeting options; people with disabilities or mental health conditions may need special considerations about venues and meeting formats. Likewise, people who identify on the autism spectrum can have sensory needs, and people with ADHD may need information presented in specific ways. The key here is to get to know your people *as* people – not just workers. There is a tendency

in many organisations to assume that everyone should be always available and ready to participate at the convenience of the managers, when in real life we all have different needs.

- Short meetings are generally better than long ones. Only have long meetings if you have a specific plan for how you're spending the time.
- It helps to have a basic agenda. An order of speakers and time limits for each report in can be sufficient. Manage the time so that the last speaker doesn't just get a minute before everyone rushes off.
- You can invite special guest presenters – these can add interest and variety to regular group meetings and seed new ideas.

Notes on remote mode

'You're on mute' … Online meetings made research possible in the pandemic so it seems churlish to complain about them, but they can be so, well, *blah*. While online meetings are convenient and easy, they are fatiguing compared to face-to-face meetings. The bad aspects of face-to-face meetings, such as people talking for too long, are magnified in an online space. Here are some tips to make your online meetings less *blah*.

- Turn off self-view. Research has shown that looking at yourself and being tempted to constantly adjust your posture, hair and chin angle is one of the things that make online meetings so tiring.
- Get into the habit of being on mute until it's your time to speak. This reduces background noise and increases clarity for people with poor connections.
- Resist the urge to private message others snarky or sarcastic comments. Most platforms have a 'save chat' function and

these supposedly private comments can show up in a log. Also, as any politician will tell you, a screen grab of a private conversation can cause havoc if it goes public.

- Have a meeting protocol for responding to speakers. It can be as simple as typing a 'q' for a question or a 'c' for comment. If you are the sort that keeps a progressive speaker list (where women are given a privileged speaking position), managing a conversation on chat can be easier than in person.
- People are often reluctant to talk first in front of a crowd, and this tendency is magnified online. In face-to-face settings, merely staying silent after asking a question is usually enough to force someone to speak. Not so online! Breakout rooms are a good tool to reduce Zoom stage fright as they give people a chance to discuss and formulate an answer together. Or use the chat function for responses – people are more likely to type than to talk to a crowd.
- People can collaborate more easily if there is a digital object they can mutually 'touch'. Platforms like Padlet or Miro, or even simple Google Docs, give people a chance to share images and text as they talk about ideas.

Further reading

There are many, many business books on meetings. Most of them deal with meetings in the context of commercial industry. There are many peculiarities of academia in terms of culture which limit the usefulness of these sources. However, we feel that *Project Management for the Unofficial Project Manager* by Kogon, Blackmore and Wood[2] has timeless and applicable advice on the whole suite of issues that arise when working in teams towards project goals, including running meetings.

Notes

1   Jean Lave and Etienne Wenger, *Situated learning: Legitimate peripheral participation*, Cambridge: Cambridge University Press, 1991.
2   Kory Kogon, Suzette Blakemore and James Wood, *Project management for the unofficial project manager*, Dallas: BenBella Books, 2015.

3 Writing an amazing email about your research

TL;DR

- Email is the lifeblood of university communications. Spend time getting your style right and it can pay big dividends.
- Anticipate your reader's communication needs and try to include as much detail in the initial email as you can, without overwhelming them.
- Keep your requests modest and connect them firmly to the expertise of the person you are addressing.
- Don't expect a quick answer. Sometimes nudging people for a response can be effective, but the timing has to be right. Don't be pushy.

In a nutshell

Email is the lifeblood of university communications: quick, easy, painless … and so easy to get wrong. There's so much we could say about how to write the perfect email, but this chapter focuses on writing emails that raise awareness of your research with someone you don't know well – or may not have met in person.

DOI: 10.4324/9781003197713-4

The art of the 'cold call' email is a key academic skill. There are a few reasons you might want to email a person you don't know about your research:

1 to seek help or feedback on your current project
2 to ask a favour, such as giving a presentation, supplying data or sending a paper that you can't access
3 to ask for a job
4 to report a problem or ask for help
5 to express admiration and make a connection.

In an academic job, you are expected to do a range of things that help out other academics and the discipline; this is called 'service work'. When you are writing an email, it helps to keep in mind that your mail is one of hundreds that an academic gets and they fall into 'genres'. By more clearly pitching your email into a genre, and (where appropriate) providing the right information in advance, you will have more chance of getting an early and positive answer.

Each email genre requires a slightly different approach. We are going to illustrate this chapter with real examples of (very poorly written) emails and show you how to do it better!

How to prepare

While we were writing this book, we asked academics on Twitter about their experiences of email and how to write a good one. We were a bit surprised at the number of complaints we got about people sending inappropriate and borderline unprofessional emails to colleagues. These academics received emails that:

1   complained about the emailer's work not being cited in a paper the academic had published
2   told the academic their theory or findings were wrong (much easier than writing a paper rebutting the original work, I suppose)
3   questioned the academic's expertise
4   asked the academic to basically write a paper or dissertation
5   asked for information about research participants (most projects will have specific ethics clearance that prevents sharing this kind of data)
6   contained legal threats.

Most of these complaints were about members of the public or more senior academics. These people are unlikely to buy this book, but it's good to know what other things end up in an academic email inbox, so you know what you are competing against for attention!

Most academics are good-natured souls who are drawn to the profession because they are helpful people. Unfortunately, most academics find their helpful instincts are hijacked by an industry determined to squeeze them for the maximum amount of work. Therefore, your request for help is going to land on a large pile of similar requests.

You are more likely to get an answer if (1) your request is modest and (2) you connect your request for help firmly with the expertise the person has to offer. Below are some examples.

How to be good at it

Seeking help or feedback

Here's how not to seek help in an email:

Dear Professor,

I am 2 years into my PhD and struggling with my analysis. I was wondering if you could take a look and give me some advice?

Regards,
Struggling Student

Here's our improved version:

Dear Professor [surname],

I'm 2 years into a PhD about employability using text analysis techniques. I'm analysing job ads using machine learning natural language processing. I'm having trouble choosing which swapped vector machines (SVMs) to use. My supervisor is not an expert in this area.

I'm writing to you because I read an excellent paper of yours called 'Using the right swapped vector machines'. I found this paper really helpful, but I was wondering what you think of 'super number one SVMs'. Do you have any insights to share? I understand you are very busy and appreciate the time you have taken to consider my request.

Regards,
Struggling Student

If you think no one writes an email like the first one, let us enlighten you: Inger gets a couple each month. Trust us, this email is not going to be answered in a hurry – if at all. You have already demonstrated you are not a great communicator. The academic may not even want to make the effort to ask you for more information because they fear getting drawn into a long, fruitless exchange. Emails like this are impossible to answer quickly and will wind up at the end of a long, unanswered list of similar requests – or get deleted.

Our improved version tells the reader exactly what help is required and why. If you can't form a really specific question at the end of an email like this (and we acknowledge this can be hard), the sentence 'Do you have any insights to share?' is a good one to use. Open-ended questions like this invite the receiver to share as much (or as little) information as they want to.

The last line indicates that you understand that you may have to wait for a reply. You might be surprised what glorious emails you will get in response if you show a bit of emotional sensitivity to the person you are writing to. We suggest you send an email like this only once. Following up repeatedly with this kind of request is unlikely to make the person more inclined to answer you.

Asking for feedback on your work from an academic you don't know is very tricky. We need to remind you that, in most countries, if you give a piece of your dissertation to someone outside of your doctoral supervisory team, you have immediately disqualified that person from being an examiner. And the pool of people you draw on for your examiners is probably pretty tiny already.

Reading and reviewing writing, especially writing from students, is a time-consuming business. Most academics have more than enough of this work to do already and have precious little time to extend this service beyond their own students. While you could write a polite email along the lines of the one provided above, we don't like your chances of getting a positive response.

We have one big exception to the above advice: when your research work is transdisciplinary. If you are using methods and/or producing results that your supervisor or collaborators cannot easily assess, it can be helpful to get another reader from that discipline. For example, Inger once supervised a person doing a PhD in musicology who was using fuzzy set theory from mathematics. Inger had no hope of understanding the maths part, and so enlisted help from colleagues in that department at her university. They were delighted to see such a novel application and gave it their seal of approval. If you are doing a PhD and need this kind of feedback, we recommend that you get your supervisor to do the approach on your behalf if possible.

Asking for data access

This is directly related to research work, so let's look at a bad example (again, this email is real!):

Dear Professor,

I saw that you used the kind of data I want to use in my PhD. Can you send it to me plz?

Thx,
Struggling Student

Data access is a difficult issue in academia – a problem that students and early-career researchers often don't think through sufficiently. It's disconcerting to start a project and realise your access to lab or field sites to gather data is restricted in some way. When you don't collect your own, you quickly find out that data is (1) not available or (2) expensive. There are also likely to be all kinds of caveats and restrictions that make it hard for even a good-natured academic to share. The advice for this email is the same as above, really: make the request both specific and modest. Our friend Dr Emily Kothe gets a lot of these requests. She suggests the person receiving your mail needs to know your bona fides and how you intend to use the data. Here is our revised version:

Dear Professor [surname],

I am a PhD student studying/working with [insert name of supervisor/collaborator].

I read an excellent paper you wrote a couple of years ago that used job ad data from Burning Glass Industries. I went to their website, but it wasn't clear how researchers can go about requesting data sets from them.

Can you share the data you used in your paper with me? If not, can you please advise how I would go about getting data from Burning Glass?

If you are willing to share, I would use the data in my thesis and a publication we are aiming at [insert name of journal]. I would need to receive the data by [date] in order to make the deadline for [your deliverable].

If you are not the person best placed to answer my request, I would appreciate being referred to the member of the team who might be able to help.

Regards,
Struggling Student

Notice the little bit of flattery in the first paragraph of our improved version? It never hurts to tell an academic you like their work. This email signals who you are working with and what you intend to do with the data. It also gives the person a deadline by which you need the data – which is important, as data can sometimes be reformatted or structured to meet the request and the person getting the email needs to know if they have time to fulfil your request.

And on a slightly tangential note, while Inger is a nicer, more forgiving person, Simon would suggest that if you really intend to use 'plz' and 'thx' in an email to a senior academic, you might also need a note from your parents to be allowed out after dark.

Asking for a job or other position

Writing an email asking for a job is a tough challenge. Look, it's a tough market out there and academic work is so niche that it's likely there will only be a few people in the world looking for talents like yours. Most research projects are short-term contracts, so writing directly to people in your field is a valid job-searching strategy. Associate Professor Ivan Kassal of the University of Sydney gets a lot of these and shared his formula for a good one. We couldn't improve on this list:

1   correct salutation
2   evidence that you read my website and know what I do
3   explanation of how your interests align with what I do
4   attached complete CV
5   proper grammar and spelling.

A PhD is kind of like a job, when you think about it. Here's a good example of someone reaching out to an academic to ask if they have any studentships available. We adapted this from a real example sent to use by an academic who was so impressed by it; they kept it as an example for their own master's students to use when applying for a PhD.

Dear Professor [surname],

My name is [name] and I am a [discipline specialist] from [country], currently working with [company] doing [job]. I also have experience in [skill set].

I am contacting you as I have recently come across your PhD scholarship opportunity at [university website]: [link to advertisement].

I completed my bachelor's degree in [discipline] from [university] in 2009 and a master's degree in [topic area] from [university] in [country] in 2013, with specialisations in [specialisations]. Please refer to [links to the programs they completed].

I wrote my master's thesis on [three-line explanation of topic]. My thesis can be accessed from [university] library here: [link to PDF].

I have won quite a few scholarships for studying, such as [insert details].

In addition to formal education, I have progressively kept myself updated on [field] by doing [informal opportunities]. Besides my passionate engagement with my [type of] career, I am a [insert hobbies, framed as pursuits, e.g., not 'photography', but 'amateur photographer'].

This PhD is a perfect opportunity for me to leverage my current knowledge, skills and experiences towards [bigger research outcome, e.g., how you want to change the world].

I have a few more questions to ask and would like to know what would be the best time to contact you?

Regards,
Curious Student

Communicating a problem: research integrity

Sometimes you will have to email someone about a research integrity matter. In our experience, people are very uninterested in learning about how to deal with research integrity matters until they encounter a huge problem, like having to accuse someone else of plagiarism – or being accused of it yourself. Needless to say, make yourself very familiar with the research integrity principles in your institution and the staff code of conduct (if there is one) so you know what your responsibilities are.

Communicating about research integrity issues is a delicate area and must be approached with extreme caution. If you make an accusation of plagiarism in writing, you need to be prepared to back it up with the right kind of evidence. We strongly suggest you seek advice from your university before reaching out so you can include the right information and make sure the email is written in a non-defamatory manner. The university may offer to reach out on your behalf – if so, we suggest you let them handle it!

This is the moment in this chapter where we remind you that EMAIL IS THE LEAST PRIVATE FORM OF COMMUNICATION THERE IS. People panic about being sued or losing their job because of something they said on social media, but someone forwarding an email with sensitive information to the wrong person can be even worse. And don't get us started on the accidental 'Cc: All' that includes a history of private conversations that others shouldn't see (hot tip – set your email to give you a 20-second delay before it sends so you have time to delete!). Our standard advice is to assume every single email, whether it's to a colleague, student or member of the public, can be forwarded to the vice-chancellor at any moment. In reality, the university owns your.edu email account anyway, so your entire email history is discoverable and May Be Used Against You in a Court of Law. If you are even slightly worried about privacy, or what you are saying in the email, use a personal account (bearing in mind you are trusting the person at the other end not to forward it to your employer or anyone else). The only really private form of communication is one to one, in person, with no recording devices present, in the middle of a football field – although even then people may hear you with the right kind of specialised equipment!

Making a connection

The best kind of email to write – and one that doesn't get much attention – is to express admiration and make a connection. Academics love to hear their work has been read *and* enjoyed. You can be sure that an email like this will always be well received. Inger is lucky enough to get between five and ten complimentary emails a week: the result of over a decade of blogging, and well over half a million published words on the topic of doing a PhD. Some are a quick thank you to say 'The

PhD is FINALLY finished!' Others are heartfelt outpourings, like this delightful excerpt:

> I've always found it natural and effortless to complain bitterly when the world, or the people in it, fail to conform completely to my complex set of needs and expectations. I have therefore made it a part of my new decade's resolutions to also express my feelings when things go well.
>
> My older, and even more repressed (in a gentlemanly, English way), brother did this when he recently told me he loved me. Actually, he emailed the sentiment, as a face to face exchange of such profound intimacy could have provoked a cardiac infarction in one or both of us. I give him great credit for saying it, though, as such validation from an older, smarter and much more successful sibling meant a huge deal to me.
>
> No don't worry, I'm not going to tell you I love you, but I would like to express my thanks for the important, but comfortably understated, role you played in helping me navigate the Dark Night of the Soul that was my PhD journey; for providing a break from the reductionist, positivist world view represented by [discipline] ... If I can summon the courage to express such sentiments verbally, I will do so next time I see you.

You don't have to be this erudite and effusive, but if you write from the heart, your recipient will need to be made of stone not to take it well.

There can be some more instrumental ways of using the complimentary email: it can be part of a publicity strategy for a paper you have written. If you have gone to the trouble of writing and publishing a paper, you might as well try to get it noticed by people who will be interested. The people you have cited are the most obvious interest group.

Publishers sometimes offer a special URL to allow a limited number of people to access the paper via open access. You may also be able to circulate a pre-print version of the paper. Use these links and pre-print copies wisely to get the paper to people who might appreciate it (and maybe even cite it in their own work). The only reason people might hesitate to answer a complimentary email like this about their work is that they want to read your paper first and don't have time. We suggest something like the following:

Dear Professor [surname],

I'm writing to thank you for your work, in particular the paper you wrote [insert details]. I work on [insert topic] and recently published a paper citing you [details]. In particular I used [part of their paper] to argue [your argument].

I know you must be busy, so don't feel compelled to read it – I just wanted to express my gratitude and let you know that your work is valued.

Notes on remote mode

This section is a bit redundant here because email is remote mode in its most pure form: asynchronous and disembodied. We only want to note that in this much more online world, the volume of email is huge and growing. It's probably impossible to measure how much email is flying around the world, but according to 99firms (not a highly reliable source but the only one we could find who would have a go!), here are some ideas of the possible scale of email communication:

- There are more than four billion email users worldwide. That's half the world's population!
- **More than three million emails are sent every second**.
- There are more than seven billion email accounts.
- Ninety-five per cent of email users check their email every day.
- Nearly 60 per cent of email users check their spam folder daily.[1]

In this high-volume email environment, it can be hard to get your email read.

The title of the email is important. You could go with something descriptive, but it might not cut through. Try email titles that trigger curiosity or be very specific about what you need. For example, an email entitled 'A copy of my latest paper' will get more attention if you include a *why*: 'A copy of my latest paper which might interest you as I have adopted a similar methodology'.

Further reading

Would anyone even read a book on email?! We are not sure. But if you feel so moved, we recommend *A World Without Email* by Cal Newport.[2] It may seem perverse to recommend a book on getting rid of email at the end of a chapter about email, but we think there is too much email in the world! Along with an interesting history of how email became the most ubiquitous form of digital communication, Newport's book has some solid recommendations on how to make less of it!

Notes

1   99Content, 'How many email users are there?', 99firms, n.d., https://99firms. com/blog/how-many-email-users-are-there/.

2   Cal Newport, *A world without email: Reimagining work in an age of communication overload*, New York: Penguin Putnam, 2021.

4 Turning your original research into lectures

TL;DR

- Lecturing is a good opportunity to hone your communication skills and key messages with a captive audience. Undergraduates need to be informed *and* entertained.
- There are different lecture structures. Consider the basic types, then plan your lecture before you develop detailed content.
- Don't launch straight into making a PowerPoint presentation. Use an activity matrix to organise your lecture content so the audience can participate.

In a nutshell

Teaching has changed a lot in the last 30 years, but the good old lecture is a teaching format that has endured for 800 years and has proved to be remarkably resilient. Inger has an old book from 1978 called *Lecturing and Explaining* by George Brown, which she rescued from a library throwaway table. This musty old tome is a surprisingly useful if slightly outdated resource and is now out of print. Brown observed lecturers' work and

DOI: 10.4324/9781003197713-5

explains their techniques in detail and why their strategies work (or not). Although this book is showing its age, the lecture formulas Brown offers have been tried and tested by your academic forebears over decades, even centuries. At the start of the book, Brown makes the point that a lecture is 'arranged around a set of key points with associated examples, illustrations, elaborations and qualifications', which is as good a definition as any.[1] He goes on to claim there are five 'ideal types' of lecture, which he developed by watching a lot of lecturers working and by looking carefully at their notes. In our opinion, these types seem to still hold true in practice.

1   **Topic-focused**. Brown calls this the 'classical' lecture. It covers an idea or set of linked themes. Generally, the lecture contains main sections of about 15 minutes in length and nested subsections that deal with various dimensions of the topic. The classic is also a kind of 'ur-structure' that often underpins the other types of lectures, so we have offered Table 4.1 to show you how to lay one out.

2   **Problem-centred**. In this lecture, a problem is stated at the start, and the lecture revolves around solutions or approaches to solving the problem. A variation on the problem-centred lecture is a *solution-oriented talk*, where you explain how a solution was developed and theorise about why it works (thanks to @tdlearning for this idea). Problem- or solution-centred lectures are often encountered in mathematics, engineering and physics, but there's no reason problem-centred talks should be confined to those disciplines: they are great for showing students how to apply all kinds of critical and creative thinking. We've seen this style adopted in the humanities with interesting results.

3   **Sequential**. This is based around a series of linked statements that reveal a cause-and-effect relationship or a historical timeline of some sort. The sequential is also good

Table 4.1 Preparing a classical-style lecture

Lecture: So you're finishing your PhD in a pandemic – what's next?

Subsection	Keys		Examples/illustrations
What is wrong with the post-PhD employment market? (10 mins)	1.	The gap between the number of academic jobs and how many people are looking for them	Word cloud about how people are feeling about the pandemic
	2.	Where people end up after their PhD when they can't find an academic job	Statistics about the linear growth of academic jobs compared to the non-linear number of people looking for them
	3.	The idea of a 'hidden job market' for researchers outside of academia (80 per cent of employers who post a research-oriented job do not use the keyword 'PhD', which means many appropriate jobs are hidden from view)	Statistics on graduate destinations – where do people go after their PhD? Screen grab from a job search using 'PhD' in a normal job search engine, which shows only academic jobs
What we tried to do about it (10 mins)	1.	Introduce the machine learning and natural language processing method	Show graphs of machine learning results for various industries so they get the abstract concepts
	2.	Describe the technology underpinning PostAc algorithm	

(Continued)

Table 4.1 continued

Lecture: So you're finishing your PhD in a pandemic – what's next?		
Subsection	*Keys*	*Examples / illustrations*
What we found out (15 mins)	1. There are more non-academic PhD-level jobs than jobs inside the academy 2. The jobs are in a range of areas, not just in data science 3. The pandemic has started to affect the composition of the job market – online shopping is data intensive, for instance	Tables and graphs of analysis of Australian and New Zealand job markets showing industries where highly research-intensive jobs are located Comparison tables of pre- and post-pandemic job market analysis
What you can do with what you know now (15 mins)	1. You have more skills than you think and your subject matter expertise can still be valuable 2. Change your attitude to professional development and start networking outside academia 3. Here are some good books to read	Analysis of skills required in academic jobs and non-academic jobs, showing the crossovers and similarities Lists of resources and books to follow up

for logical reasoning in disciplines like philosophy. This style is favoured in the humanities but can be used to good effect in the sciences and/or creative disciplines.

4   **Comparative**. In this lecture, two or more systems, processes or histories are presented in relation to each other. The purpose of the comparative lecture is to tease out

oppositions like similarities and differences or advantages and disadvantages. We see this structure adopted less frequently, perhaps because there is a lot of creative intellectual work required to construct one, but it's often highly effective and memorable.

5   **Thesis**. This begins with an assertion of a fact or position, which is then supported with a range of evidence and examples. In a way, your viva or oral exam follows this basic structure. We question whether this style is the best for the undergraduate classroom where the task is less about convincing and more about educating.

How to prepare

We think it is helpful to decide what kind of lecture you want to deliver from the list above before you do anything else; each of the types implies some kind of specific prep work to assemble all the materials you need. It's tempting to jump straight in and start making PowerPoint slides, but if you do this, it's likely your lecture will be too long and lack structure. We suggest outlining a lecture, using a table format like the one shown in Table 4.1. In this case, each of the subsections has themes with a rough delivery time; within each of the sections are Brown's 'keys', with a column on the right to marshal the list of resources required. This outline can then inform your slides and script. Start with one slide for each key, then expand the number of slides if they become too crowded.

How to be good at it

The trick with giving a great lecture is building in the audience participation from the start. The previous section showed you how to plan what you are going to say, but it's even better if you plan in the interaction the audience will have with you, and with each other. Again, a table is a great planning tool to ensure that you put on a good show and keep to time. Table 4.2 gives an example of an 'activity matrix' in a format that Inger uses for all her workshops and lectures. This one is for a class about social media based on content in the book she wrote with Deborah Lupton and Pat Thomson, *The Digital Academic*.[2]

The activity matrix forces you to think about what your audience is doing at each moment. In Table 4.2, Inger breaks up the lecture into smaller sections, in line with a classical topic-based lecture structure, but each one has an audience activity keyed to the topic. She lists what the presenter is doing and what the participants are doing in each block of time. If the participant column only contains 'listen', the lecture will not be very engaging. Table 4.2 shows how you might find ways for the audience to interact with each other, to do something or to react to the content being presented.

- The lecture is the easiest of our presentation formats to convert to online mode, as it is similar to a straight-to-camera talk anyway. However, even basic conference software offers plenty of opportunities to engage your audience in what you are presenting. Try polls or shared whiteboards as part of your audience interaction.
- Use the chat function to give students a chance to talk to each other and reflect on the content of your lecture.
- Online polling software is easier to run in an online space, and there is a wide variety of options to deliver different kinds of interactive polls. For example, put a poll at the end of a Zoom session, as people exit, to get feedback or testimonials from your students. The poll can be as simple as a couple of questions. Inger's team uses the following three questions:

Table 4.2 Planning for audience interaction in a lecture

Lecture series: Social media for academics

Session 1: Identity (7 August)

Time	Presenter	Participants	Resources
2:00–2:15 pm	Warm-up and briefing about identity issues for academics in online spaces	Feeling on a Post-it note exercise	Multicoloured Post-its or Padlet Textas Name tags
2:15–2:30 pm	Introduce digital resident and visitor maps concept Show online video	Use Mentimeter poll tool so people can locate themselves on visitor/resident matrix	Big Post-it notes, Padlet or Miro board Textas Emoji stickers
2:30–3:30 pm	Talk about styling your online biography and 'dressing' your websites	Five-minute writing exercise	Link to Tamson's bio as an example of what you can do
3:30–4:00 pm	Discuss the problems of platform capitalism	Listen, take notes, discuss the concepts in breakout rooms	

1　What did you like about this lecture?
2　What would you like to know more about?
3　Would you recommend this lecture to other people?

These three simple questions can form the backbone of an evaluation strategy for your teaching and generate testimonials you can use in a promotion application.

- Breakout rooms can be created to let people discuss the aspects of the lecture as a small group, which makes it easy to run 'pair and share' exercises of all kinds.

- There's usually a hands-up or Q&A function that facilitates question taking – in our experience, question sessions are even easier to run in online spaces than in big lecture halls, where people may be reluctant to put up their hand and have everyone turn and look at them.

Further reading

There are many books on teaching out there, but many of them are, frankly, a little uninspiring and a bit earnest. Researchers in the area of education (including Inger!) tend to write earnest, research-informed critiques of higher education rather than helpful 'to do' texts. One exception is *Teaching What You Don't Know* by Therese Huston.[3] This book is designed to help you solve the common problems that occur when you have to teach a new class at short notice. Early career researchers often 'inherit' the course notes and structures of other staff and have to quickly whip up 12 lectures in two weeks. Teaching this way is nerve wracking because you may not have a deep background in the subject and be fighting all semester to stay a week ahead of where your students are. Huston reassuringly walks you through this difficult task, but the advice about making difficult information accessible surprisingly applicable to many other kinds of teaching situations.

Notes

1   George Brown, *Lecturing and explaining*, London: Methuen, 1978, p. 62.
2   Deborah Lupton, Inger Mewburn and Pat Thomson, *The digital academic: Critical perspectives on digital technologies in higher education*, London: Routledge, 2017.
3   Therese Huston, *Teaching what you don't know*, Cambridge, MA: Harvard University Press, 2009.

5 Talking about your research in social settings

TL;DR

- Yes, despite its reputation, academia is a very social profession, and no, you can't avoid the socialising (sorry).
- Just shut up: listening is more effective than talking to build trusted connections.
- Don't be a bore and lecture people about your research in social settings, even if they ask you about it. Have a simple sentence or 'logline' that describes your research in an intriguing way. Test-drive this sentence and refine it as you go.
- Recognise different types of conversational gambits and 'troubles talk' common to the academic conversational repertoire.
- Use social media to create your own tea room vibe.

In a nutshell

Despite its reputation as a haven for introverts, academia is a very social profession. It helps your career enormously if you become adept at talking to people in semi-formal professional settings. Our shorthand for this type of social space is 'tea rooms'

DOI: 10.4324/9781003197713-6

because food and drink are often present. These are definitely professional settings where business is contracted, but it's mixed in with general social chit-chat. Think of the 4 pm Friday lab drinks or the dreaded wine-and-cheese evenings that seem to pass for fun on campus.

Semi-formal spaces like tea rooms are more common than you might think. A variation on the tea room is the so-called 'corridor track' of conferences. As you know, conference presentations are clustered in sub-topics, and at before-COVID conferences the same room would be used for each sub-topic throughout the conference. These were represented as 'tracks' in the program. Tracks are a good way to navigate large conferences. You can meet people with similar interests by following the same track all the way through the conference, but there's not much chance to talk in the rooms. The 'corridor track' happens outside these formal presentation spaces, where people gather to chat outside the rooms. All sorts of things start in the corridor track: invitations to collaborate, writing projects and even 'the job interview you have before the actual job interview' where people informally sound you out on your skill set and experience.

Show us a successful academic and nine times out of ten we will show you a socially confident person, comfortable in a range of settings. Tea room talk is an opportunity to get to know people socially, which builds the social trust necessary for trading information about people, resources and opportunities. But the tea room in academic life is not easy for everyone; carers often have less time for mingling, especially after hours, or and there are people who are uncomfortable with free-form social settings, full of people they don't know very well and no clear 'rules' for interacting.

When you become a research student, you are suddenly allowed access to the staff tea room, a place that becomes more and more familiar as you progress to being a postdoc and/or a member of teaching staff. If you are finding this aspect of academia difficult, don't worry too much. Unfortunately, we can't teach you to be more socially adept and comfortable in these situations – it's a set of skills most of us spend a lifetime learning. Most people need help socialising in academia because, well, it can be an awkward kind of place. When you are an undergraduate, you only encountered academics in the classroom or during brief moments in the café queue. The academic tea room can be a whole new level of awkward, so we thought we would include a short section highlighting the importance of these spaces and some advice on navigating this new social challenge.

How to prepare

We could have made this chapter all about listening. The more you listen to people, the more they tend to like you, but good listening needs to be active. Most of us believe we are better listeners than we actually are. Here's a (non-exhaustive) list of listening tips.

- Resist your natural urge to interrupt and try giving people at least three times as long to make their point. Giving people space to fully express themselves will make you a more comfortable conversationalist.
- Lean forward slightly when people talk to you. This is a common, non-verbal way of showing attention, as is eye contact, but...
- Continuous, direct eye contact can be intimidating. Go for short but frequent glances. If you have trouble making and maintaining eye contact, look at people's ears or the frames of their glasses.
- Noises like *mm-hmm* and words like 'yeah' can encourage people to keep speaking, but too much of it can be

interpreted as asking someone to stop. A nod can be more effective.

- You need to listen, but also signal you have listened. The easiest way is to reflect back some content of what the person said to you in your conversational response. This is easier said than done. Pay attention next time you are in a social setting, and you will notice that many people are bad at this obvious step in the listening process. Worse, some people are completely unaware of how little they appear to listen. Which people? I'm just going to say it: culturally, men are let off the hook on this aspect of conversation more than women. Showing genuine interest in what the other person is saying is not just a woman thing, but is the key reason why women are often framed as better communicators in the workplace.

- Asking questions is an easy way to signal you have heard what the person said, but you can also share a similar story or extrapolate from their point. Resist the urge to offer advice and 'fix' other people's problems. Instead, commiserate and/or ask the person what they plan to do about the problem. Try banning the use of the word 'should' for a week, and take note of how often you have to stop yourself.

- Make note of what people talk about – it shows you what is important to them. Remember these details for future interactions. If you meet a lot of people, consider investing in a contacts database (used in a non-creepy way of course!).

How to be good at it

'What is your research about?' is the most common conversational opener when you meet someone for the first time in a tea room setting. Just remember this conversational gambit is small talk, not an invitation to give a lecture. Have a one-sentence answer handy for this situation – preferably one that makes people want to talk to you more. In the movie business, this kind of sentence is called a logline.

Here's the logline for the movie *Jaws*: 'When a killer shark unleashes chaos on a beach community, a local sheriff, a marine biologist, and an old seafarer must hunt the beast down before it kills again.'

A movie logline has both the characters and the plot line: these two ingredients can be redrawn in research terms. For instance, Inger's PhD logline was 'I'm studying how architects talk with their hands so I can work out what gesture is doing in the classroom'. The character was 'architects' and the plot was 'What is gesture doing?' Your logline will probably change from time to time. For the last five years, Inger has been studying post-PhD employability – but this is a topic, not a logline. When asked about her research, she now says, 'I'm trying to teach machines how to read job advertisements so we can find out how many jobs there for researchers outside universities'. The characters are algorithms (machines) and early-career researchers, and the plot is a mystery story about the search for jobs.

The logline is a tease – you are not trying to explain exactly what you are doing but give people an easy opening to ask questions if they want to. The logline is just a tool to show people you are an interesting person doing interesting research. Being interesting is an important but little recognised cultural asset for a researcher.

Join conversations

Free-form conversations about research can be difficult, even if you are a confident extrovert like Inger. Tea rooms do not have well-defined interaction structures, like lectures or presentations, so unpacking the hidden rules is a bit trickier. A big room full of people you don't know all that well can be confronting, but there's a trick to inserting yourself into conversations. Generally, people can sustain a conversation in groups of up to four. If more than four people are standing in a cluster, one person is usually 'holding the floor', probably by telling a story of some kind. To avoid finding yourself standing awkwardly on the margins of an existing group, use simple maths. Approach someone standing on their own first – they are probably keen to have someone to talk to. If people are in groups, approach the groups of two – they are the most likely to be open to an extra conversational partner. And, if you go up to a group of four, it's highly likely you will 'break' the group up, but until you do, you'll never know if you're an intrusive newcomer or a welcome break!

Develop conversational repertoires

While there is a surprising amount of conversation analysis research, there is precious little about conversations between academics in these informal settings (Inger published one of the very few academic papers on the topic).[1] However, between us we've had more than 45 years of immersion in academic life. (We also did some 'research' by asking people on Twitter, which confirmed many of our assumptions!) There is a certain amount of predictability in these conversations, at least in terms of topic and structure. It's possible to identify a few conversational gambits and develop 'repertoires' for responding in the moment. In fact, we advise making a study of these situations and practising your tea room game whenever you can.

Here are some conversational gambits we have noticed and some ideas for dealing with each one.

- **'What are you working on?'** is a nice polite way to start a conversation with anyone, so you should always be prepared for it. Don't treat this conversational gambit as an invitation to bore for your country – use your logline! A good logline can prompt people to ask questions and help the conversation along. Don't forget to turn the question back on your conversation partner so you don't monopolise the whole conversation, which leads us to our second most popular conversational gambit …

- **'Let me bore you with my research.'** This is a common response when people are asked what they are working on. Honestly, we don't know why people can lose sight of conversation being a two-way deal, but many academics go into 'lecture mode' when asked about their research. Listening politely is sometimes the only option, but inviting someone else into the conversation can be a way to open it up and divert the flow a bit. Or manufacture a need to go to the bathroom, in a pinch!

- **'Here's how we did it in the old days.'** (Variation: 'Let me tell you why it was better.') A firm favourite of the older generations, particularly when there is more than one person of a certain age present. Both of us have been guilty of this one too! Academia has an age hierarchy, so it can be a career-limiting move to just blank the old person and move on. Personally, we feel there can be a lot to learn from listening to old-timers, so try to turn the conversation onto an area you are interested in by asking questions. For instance, 'What was it like to research before journals were online?' or 'Did you have any useful note-taking strategies that might still work for me?'

- **'Why don't you do that the way I would do it?'** This is when someone listens to your research approach and suggests a different way to do something, tacitly ignoring or dismissing what you have already done. It can be annoying to have all your hard work dismissed, but try not to be defensive. Listen with an open heart and ask questions – but try not to let other people's certainty knock your confidence in your own ideas and approaches. Even if the person is offering the 'advice' as a pure dominance move (and some people do), remember that everyone is a potential audience and their comments are a good window into what's going on in other people's heads when they hear your ideas. Take it as an opportunity to make notes for your next presentation!

- **'Help! What would you do about x?'** Genuine cries for help from colleagues are rare but delightful, and we think they are to be encouraged. True scholarly dialogue is something to be treasured, but we feel we must warn you that there is a variation of this kind of conversational gambit where people try to suck you into spending time helping them. This help can be in the form of reading over drafts or even sorting out technical problems. We are fine with helping others. Certainly, there are many advantages to being generous with your time and expertise … so long as it doesn't become a huge time burden to you. We've noticed that young women in particular can be hooked into helping more senior colleagues without appropriate recognition and recompense.

- **'Have you seen the preprint by X about Y?'** (Thanks @quantum_graeme.) This is usually an attempt to open a conversation about a new area of research. If you haven't read the paper, it's easy enough to get the person to tell you about it. This kind of conversational gambit can sometimes be a dominance move – knowledge is currency in academia, and demonstrating you are up with the latest is a form of jostling for status. We find it best to just treat the question at face value, either way.

- **'Can you watch my practice presentation?'** (Thanks @Zelda_Doyle.) Direct requests for help and support, we think, should always be met with generosity as far as possible.

Refer to what we said about research meetings and working together as generating positive word of mouth.

- **'Were you in [meeting]? Let's discuss all the things that we *really* thought about it.'** This is a fine invitation to academic gossip, especially about management. Be careful! If you really trust the person and have feelings to share, have at it. Otherwise, we recommend it's time to change the subject.

Variations include the following.

- **Gossip**. Talking about other people and their achievements, behaviour and motivations is the lifeblood of academia. No campus could function properly without gossip because it is so strongly hierarchical; gossip offers a way to manage around powerful people who might abuse their position or authority. Gossip, especially about people's behaviour, is a complex human need and can be the source of valuable social knowledge you need to survive and thrive – especially if it steers you away from bullies. It can also be a powerful way to build bonds because to be invited into gossip is usually a sign of trust – but it's tricky to get the gossip piece just right. We could spend a whole book on the topic! So we can only suggest that you must find your own comfort level. If you are at all unsure about whether or not to participate in an invitation to gossip, either because of the person you are talking to or because of the subject of the gossip, just stay out of it!
- **Mansplaining**. Refer to our section on answering questions and dealing with trolls at the back of the book for specific advice on this one!
- **'F★^k I'm good, just ask me' (aka FIGJAM)**. Basically, this is when people are just showing off by telling you all about their achievements as a form of dominance behaviour. While we think there is a sad lack of celebration in academia,

it can be hard to be talked at. Excusing yourself to refill your drink can sometimes be the only way out.

- **Competitive busyness**. This is where people talk about how much they have on their plate and how overwhelmed they are. Sadly, in academia this is likely to be entirely true, but it can be a bit of a vicious cycle where people try to out-compete each other for being busier, which just makes everyone more stressed. We mention this one not so much to help you do anything about it, but so you are aware that it can contribute to a culture of overwork where you feel you need to be busy in order to be a legitimate member of the community.

Manage 'troubles talk'

People complain to each other in academic tea rooms. All. The. Time. The complaints range from bitching about paperwork to slanderous attacks on the characters of other colleagues. It can be a bit shocking to the first timer how much bitching and whining goes on in tea rooms and difficult to know how to respond. It's tempting to see this kind of 'troubles talk' as a sign of low morale or a sick research culture, but the research on troubles talk tells a more interesting, nuanced story of human bonding in action. Sharing troubles is a way of demonstrating trust and envelops us in a warm glow of shared experience.

There are ways to leverage troubles talk for these benefits, rather than descending in a spiral of negativity and gossip. In her seminal paper on the topic of troubles talk, Gail Jefferson catalogued three standard reactions: (1) diagnose the trouble, (2) offer advice and (3) share a similar trouble.[2] The safest of these strategies, in our opinion, is to share a similar trouble. Always trying to 'fix' people's troubles is annoying when what they really want is to be heard.

Or just change the subject!

Notes on remote mode

There is no doubt that the best virtual replacement of the casual academic tea room encounter is social media. Sure, social media can be a toxic slew of algorithmically poisoned content and screaming trolls, but it can also be a place to create your own tea room vibe.

The conversational 'rules' that work in social media are surprisingly similar to the ones we have offered above. Listen more than you talk and make sure you reflect the content of other people's talk in your response.

The key difference between the two modes is the way you start conversations. There is no space here to do justice to the huge topic of interacting on social media, so here are a few tips.

- Consider carefully how you 'dress' your social media handle. The pictures and words you use will clue people into what to expect from you.
- You don't need to use a picture of yourself. For nearly a decade, Inger has been a big pile of paper on Twitter. She has no doubt this is the reason why she's experienced less sexism than other female academics, but don't feel like you have to hide yourself away to avoid the trolls. Just block them. We've got more tips at the end of the book in our section on answering questions and dealing with trolls. Sometimes Simon uses a picture of himself – desperately trying to look like a rakish, cosmopolitan man about town – and other times he just gives in and looks like a clapped-out old typewriter. Depends on his mood really.
- Curate your feed of people carefully. Use search terms and hashtags to find people who share similar interests and follow them.

- Observe the talk between others carefully. What seem to be the acceptable topics and ways to respond in that particular community?
- Dip your toe in cautiously by responding to others who are having interesting conversations. Try to be useful and/or interesting if being witty is too hard.

Further reading

Unfortunately, we don't really improve our ability to socialise by reading books – in fact, you could say too much book reading got us into trouble in the first place… But if you are after something to read, the only other book we've found that treats academic tea room skills seriously is *Ms. Mentor's New and Ever More Impeccable Advice for Women and Men in Academia* by Emily Toth.[3] The book is a compendium of amazing advice for navigating the politically tricky corners of academia, with the advice amusingly framed in the form of an 'agony aunt' newspaper column where Toth answers questions and solves problems sent in by anxious academic readers.

Notes

1 Inger Mewburn, 'Troubling talk: Assembling the PhD candidate', *Studies in Continuing Education* 33, no. 3 (2011): 321–32, https://doi.org/10.1080/0158037X.2011.585151.

2 Gail Jefferson, 'On the sequential organization of troubles-talk in ordinary conversation', *Social Problems* 35, no. 4 (1988): 418–41, https://doi.org/10.2307/800595.

3 Emily Toth, *Ms. Mentor's new and ever more impeccable advice for women and men in academia*, Philadelphia: University of Pennsylvania Press, 2008.

Part II

Thinking bigger

Life extends outside the walls of academia, even though it doesn't always feel that way … In this part of the book, we explore the various formats for 'research impact'. These are presentation types that happen mostly within academic settings but are aimed at communicating research findings with people outside your immediate discipline or research field. We're quite amused by the term 'impact'; it always conjures visions of explosions in action movies. Research impact doesn't have to be on the scale of the meteor that killed the dinosaurs; most impact activities are relatively low key. They take the form of presentations to colleagues at conferences or to groups of interested stakeholders or community members. Research communication of this kind can have lasting, positive effects.

There's a growing list of competitions and opportunities to support skill development for research impact activities. Generally speaking, we think this trend towards broadening audiences is a good thing, but we have noticed these presentation types tend to cause a lot of anxiety. The presentation scenarios in this part of the book are all ones you will encounter inside the academy, or on the 'fringes' of the academy, in spaces like conferences and workshops. Here you will be talking to people who will not know you, or your research, and perhaps

DOI: 10.4324/9781003197713-7

will not have the same background as you. Lightening talks, producing posters and delivering conference talks can be confronting, but get easier with practice and preparation. This section of the book will help you develop the confidence to get out and about with your research.

6 Lightning talks

TL;DR

- Whether it's a formal talk like a Three Minute Thesis presentation or an off-the-cuff explanation, you will need to have 'ready-to-go' short talks prepared for many occasions.
- Get to the point – time is of the essence. Concentrate on one or two key points at most and make them the most interesting ones.
- Practise! But don't try to be perfect. Endeavour instead to be interesting and memorable.

In a nutshell

A lightning talk can be a talk to a mixed audience of our peers – such as a meetup where academics and professional practitioners get together. Or it can be to non-experts who know nothing about the research at all. As we pointed out earlier in the book, even academics in closely related fields may find your research hard to understand as it's by nature novel and new. Treat the lightning talk as an opportunity to explain expert-level concepts and ideas to non-experts, recognising that some will be slightly more expert than others.

DOI: 10.4324/9781003197713-8

The format of a lightning talk can be spontaneous ('Now, Inger; why don't you tell us where you're up to with the Ken Behrens Project?') or a highly structured prepared presentation to a pre-decided format – for example, a 'PechaKucha' where you have a given number of pre-prepared slides and your eye very much on the stopwatch. Either way, lightning talks are a part of your academic life and are very good exercises in thinking on your feet and performing in public. The most common formal lightning talks you'll come across these days are in competitive events like the Three Minute Thesis competition or Falling Walls, and structured public presentations like the TED Talk and all its distant cousins.

Any trainer in communication worth their salt will drum into you that no two audiences are the same, and no two speaking occasions are the same. But you can be prepared for anything by thinking through how your research can be made relatable and accessible.

How to prepare

With the content of your lightning talk, no matter what the style, format or setting, the key factor is timing. Your audience will have very little time within which to be impressed by your brilliance, so you need to do two things: first, you need to get to the point; second, you need to choose which point you are going to get to. It's highly likely you will only have enough time to get one point across. Seriously. Two if you're really good. But no more. For someone who is accustomed to dashing off the odd 80,000-word thesis or two, this is a big challenge.

If you want to try the Three Minute Thesis competition or a TED Talk, you need to get your head around the demands of the format. All lightning talks require a structured way of speaking, but competitive speaking events like the Three

Minute Thesis also ask you to conform to very strict rules and regulations. And not only will they be unlike any other set of rules or guidelines within which you will ever have to speak, but if you fail to obey them, there won't just be a spot of tut-tutting and a raising of eyebrows; rather, it's highly likely that you'll be shown the door.

So, ask yourself: what is the one thing that will grab the audience's attention and have them hanging off your every word? If you're unsure what is most interesting in your research (and this can be a bit of a daunting question early on), think about all the times you've talked about your research. This means the conversations you've had with peers, colleagues and fellow academics, and also the wildly informal occasions like family reunions when you've been cornered by a slightly ine-briated cousin who's asked you what you're up to these days. Think about what your audience's reactions were. Remember when their eyes lit up? That's probably a good point to try to get across. And that time when their eyes glazed over? That one, not so much.

Treat every event in your calendar as a potential speaking engagement so that, when the head of the department turns to you out of the blue at the end of a meeting and says, 'Well, looks like we still have five minutes left; how about you update us on your progress?', you'll be completely unfazed and come back with: 'Sure, Brian, I'd love to.' People often worry they will say something wrong when put on the spot, particularly with respect to data and measurements. Relax. You don't have to know everything. Memorise the most interesting statistics or facts. The best sort to pull out are ones that run counter to 'common sense' ideas about your topic. As a researcher, you will hear people say wrong things all the time, so make a list of these common falla-cies as a starting point for the type of fact or statistic you should memorise. By remembering only a few of the most interesting and thought-provoking facts, you become memorable yourself.

Without wishing to state the obvious, practice is the best way to get good at giving lightning talks. Getting out in front of audiences as often as possible, and becoming comfortable with all eyes being on you while you cast all modesty aside and talk about yourself, is what you need to do. And doing this with as wide a variety of audiences as possible helps. A lot. Which means you should actually seek out opportunities to talk about your work. This, of course, horrifies most researchers but the ability to give good lightning talks can determine whether you get picked for a coveted role in the faculty, whether your project gets the grant it desperately needs or whether you get funded to represent your department at a high-profile conference in a faraway, exotic land.

But always remember: you are not practising to become perfect. That whole 'practice makes perfect' thing is a myth. We are all humans – humans are warm, fuzzy and, above all, highly fallible. We can *never* be perfect. So, remind yourself that you just need to practise *so that you don't get it wrong* – there's no point in putting unnecessary and unrealistic pressure on yourself to be perfect. Especially as you can't.

How to be good at it

Thinking about your work in terms of short grabs or sound bites or even bullet points is a great way of honing your skills. Of course, for formal occasions you'll still need to be able to come up with well-reasoned, beautifully written or spoken paragraphs that describe your research at length and in great detail, but try the exercise of thinking up 10-to-15-word answers to questions like:

- What are you researching?
- What are you hoping to achieve?
- What did you do today?

You don't need to do this out loud, but do it often in your head – keep testing yourself. And, if you want to get really good at it, give yourself different audiences to address your answers to – how would you change the answer to the question if your audience was the vice-chancellor, a colleague, a school group visiting your lab or even the aforementioned cousin at the family get-together?

Turn the abstract into the concrete

To truly master the lightning talk format, you will need to provide complex explanations in very compressed way. It's helpful to have canned phrases ready to roll from your more prepared talks. Try this exercise.

1   List the frameworks, functions, systems, methods or themes that are important to your work, for example 'gene therapy' or 'auto-ethnography'.

2   Try to turn these abstract concepts into concrete analogies and metaphors. Concrete means things you can see, hear, smell, touch or taste. For example, instead of saying 'the average length of snakes in our sample set was 3000 millimetres', try 'The average length of these snakes was 3 metres, which is the same as the distance between the floor and the ceiling in most houses.'

3   Look at your list of abstract ideas and concepts. Can you relate any of them to a concrete object, like a car, plant, machine or building, or a process, like tending crops or making bread? When you have a concrete object or process in mind, write the concept up as a short statement in the following format: [abstract idea or concept] is like [concrete thing] except [conditions].

Like so:

> Our machine learning natural language processing algorithm **is like a** crop-monitoring drone. It autonomously scans the ground and works out where crops are growing well and where they are growing poorly. **Except** the crops are research-intensive job advertisements that might be suitable for PhD students.

Once you have a couple of good analogies under your belt, you will always have a pre-made shortcut to explaining complex ideas quickly. The more you put your mind to work on finding metaphors and analogies, the more they will come to you – often at inconvenient times, like in the shower. Make a habit of writing down good ones as you think of them, and listen hard for analogies that others use. Appropriate the good ones. All creativity involves some element of theft!

Pinpoint the 'WIFM'

Most audiences don't really remember what you said – they remember how you made them feel. And the most powerful emotion in the world is 'What's in it for me?' (WIFM). With a Three Minute Thesis or TED Talk, most audiences want to feel hope. The feeling that there are clever people working on complex problems is very reassuring in a complex, unpredictable world. In a faculty meeting, the dean's WIFM is that you are doing interesting, novel work that is likely to bring in some cash. Work out the WIFM and key your talk appropriately.

Find your crew

With all lightning talks, especially the competitive Three Minute Thesis–style events, getting a pit crew or support team together will give you a huge advantage. Find yourself two, three or, at most, four like-minded souls who appreciate what you are going through and are maybe even doing the same themselves but who – very importantly – are *not* from your field. The human brain is very good at filling in gaps. So, if you're a nuclear physicist and miss a vital detail while giving a presentation, if your audience are also nuclear physicists, chances are high that they won't even notice, their brains having helpfully filled in the missing detail without them even realising. But do the same thing to an audience of historians, biologists or linguists, and you'll have a sea of puzzled faces in front of you. A few external ears and eyes can help you graduate from 'OK presenter' to 'consummate performer' almost overnight.

Perform

And the key word here is 'performer'– while there is an element of performance at play every time you stand in front of people and speak, the lightning talk is probably about as theatrical you can get as a researcher. Which means, not only should you practise public speaking in general, for every occasion on which you are called upon to speak, you should probably also rehearse beforehand and warm up on the day. There are plenty of resources, both printed and online, about how actors prepare for a performance (try starting with Hamlet and his advice to 'Speak the speech, I pray you … trippingly on the tongue …'); you really could do a lot worse than learn from the world of the theatre or even stand-up comedy.

Further reading

As we said in our section on talking about research in the tea-room, reading will only take us so far when it comes to improving our improvisation skills. So we will not recommend further reading here, but we do recommend you jump on YouTube and look at some of the thousands of videos of people presenting research for inspiration. The best place to start is with videos of 3MT performances (Inger humbly suggests you have a look at The Australian National University 3MT channel as her university has a great record of winning and placing in the Asia Pacific finals). We also suggest you watch TED Talks, which are really top notch examples of taking complex issues and breaking them down into an easily digestible 20-minute format. And you could take a look at how they are using theatrical improvisation training at the Alan Alda Center for Communicating Science. Lately there has been a trend of quick science videos on TikTok, many of which are worth a look too.

Notes on remote mode

- While it's still much harder to be ambushed with the impromptu lightning talk online, it can still happen. But if you've already anticipated this, it shouldn't faze you.
- Not only will you be unfazed, but you'll have all sorts of documents and memory aids open on your screen that you can discreetly refer to while you look straight into the camera and give a beautifully prepared 'spontaneous' presentation. Inger has a row of Post-its with key nuggets of data and analogies ready to roll.
- With the more regulated lightning talks, you will undoubtedly receive reams of information about how to present to

help you stay on track so there's less room to manoeuvre. Just make sure the practice and rehearsal match the performance.

- If you know the event you are scheduled to take part in has moved online, make sure you and your pit crew do your preparations online too. Ideally, you want your support team to sit in a separate room and critique your performance on screen, rather than watching you in person and trying to imagine how well you'll come across on camera.

7 Poster presentations

TL;DR

- Use a pre-built template to lay out your poster (unless you happen to be a communications designer, of course). Always use a horizontal (landscape) format so people don't have to stoop to read your text.
- Resist the urge to crowd your poster with every detail of your research: you should still try to tell a story. Leverage people's tendency to read from left to right and down a column. Keep text between 500 and 1,000 words so that people can read the whole thing within 5 minutes.
- Employ no more than three typefaces per poster and please avoid Times New Roman! Type size should be at least 14 pt for body copy. Your headings should be at least 2 pt larger than your body copy. Subheads can be the same size as body copy but make them bold.
- Digital posters are becoming more common as conferences move into blended online/face-to-face mode. Similar principles apply to print and digital posters: don't try to crowd too much information in, and give people time to process what they have read and seen.

DOI: 10.4324/9781003197713-9

In a nutshell

A poster is a good, low-stress starting point for your conference career, as most posters are not peer reviewed and you don't have to get on stage and defend your ideas. Posters are often displayed in halls and foyers where there is a lot of foot traffic, so it's likely that more people will see a poster than hear a verbal presentation. Traditionally, posters have been between A3 and A1 size paper format. Lately, it's become fashionable to have digital posters displayed on screens. Digital posters might be a static page or a short, animated poster with voice-over (don't forget the subtitles so the poster is accessible to all).

At a conference, you can probably count on the audience sharing a common set of research interests, but they may not share a disciplinary background. You should plan for most of them to be unfamiliar with the specifics of your research, so include descriptions of methods but use diagrams and simple explanations to help people understand what you did.

Doing a great poster is surprisingly hard. Since you are not always physically present when people encounter your work, your poster carries a large communicative burden. The poster reading experience is more like being at an art gallery than reading a book.

Digital posters are a trend that has emerged in recent years as digital screens have become cheaper and ubiquitous. A digital poster can take two forms: a static image that is shown for a short period, anywhere up to 3 or 4 minutes, or a short film, with or without sound. Both these formats have different technical considerations. Both types can easily be produced in PowerPoint or a similar product, such as Keynote for Mac.

A poster should be thought about as a piece of advertising collateral that has the potential to travel beyond the conference hall. A great poster will be photographed and shared online. We recommended having a more detailed handout, staged close to your poster, which people can take away with them. The good old QR code has made a dramatic comeback during the pandemic, so make sure you include one that takes people back to a digital handout (this can be as simple as a document on a public server). Whatever the format, this handout should be beautifully written and include all your contact details. Clip a business card to it if you must – or, better still, include your contact details and webpage if you have one. Forgetting to include a takeaway means missing a fantastic self-promotion opportunity. You never know where that piece of paper will end up – maybe in the hands of someone who wants to give you a job.

How to prepare

It goes without saying that most of us are *not* communications designers. Digital tools make the process of laying out a poster so much easier, but this does not mean you have the design eye needed to make a great one. There are literally hundreds of templates on the internet that you can download, or you can use a service like Canva, which will produce a great-looking poster in next to no time. Trust others to do this work and get on with the truly difficult bit: content.

Your poster must tell the story of your research (or part of it) with images and text. Text will do most of the work but consider the context it is being read in. Sometimes people cut and paste text directly from their thesis draft, which is almost always a bad idea. Your audience is likely to be distracted and in a noisy environment, so aim for a conversational tone that is more like a magazine article than a research paper. At the very least your poster should contain an abstract that describes the purpose of the work. Write this as plainly as you can.

Most people put far too much text on a poster because they make the mistaken assumption there is a lot of room that needs to be 'filled'. Most people can read about 200 words a minute. If you want them to spend 5 minutes with your poster, this means no more than 1,000 words at most. Less is more in this instance – resist the urge to tell the passers-by everything. The idea is to provoke interest and questions, not tell the whole story of your research. And, in a design sense, there is nothing wrong with a bit of good old 'negative space' with nothing in it.

Your poster must accommodate multiple people reading it at the same time, so breaking the text up into different columns that people can move past is a good idea. However, many posters end up with a lot of disconnected bits of text on them because the author hasn't thought enough about the 'story' that holds it together. You can use standard story structures to create logical ties between each part, such as a timeline or steps in a process. Make it easy for yourself by arranging the bits of text to take advantage of the way English speakers tend to read (and write): from left to right and top to bottom. Remember we have all been trained to look at the top right of webpages, so this corner can be useful for putting information like your name and university affiliation. Remember that it's hard to read detailed text at the bottom of a poster and hold a cup of tea at the same time, so don't make people bend down to read the text. Avoid this problem by making your all your posters horizontal (landscape) format.

Images are great to illustrate your text and provide interest, but trying to emphasise everything usually means emphasising nothing. One of your images should be the 'hero' – it should be eye catching and bigger than all the rest. The purpose of the hero image is to seduce people to your poster, so it should speak about the project in some way.

How to be good at it

You will spend at least some of the time in front of your poster, talking to people, so remember all the tips we gave you about talking to colleagues in our chapter on tea rooms. Sticking to the principle of tuning into people so you can have good conversations, and the importance of listening carefully, will serve you well here.

It's important to note that people are reading poster text at two scales: from far away and close up. You should aim for no more than three kinds of typeface: one for the title, a second subheading style and then body copy for reading. You will need to have a few headlines to guide people around the page, but not so many that they compete with each other – hierarchy is important. Use images sparingly – more on that later in the book – and consider what purpose they serve. Images aren't mere decoration, they should serve a communicative purpose, but remember that every image adds more 'noise' to your poster. Excess noise, at the expense of 'signal', can make your poster hard to interpret. Image placement is a complex issue, so don't be tricky with angles unless you feel confident. If in doubt, simply line images up to imaginary grid lines.

Be consistent with how you use text. Start with 14 pt font for body text. Subheadings can be the same size, but bold. Headings should be at least 2 pt larger than the body text but be sure to test it out in a full-scale mock-up and see how it looks. Remember that text is easier to read if it's flush left and ragged on the right (i.e., not justified to both sides, which can create unsightly 'rivers' down the paragraphs). There is much less space for text on a digital poster, so plan for only 300 words or less.

You will need high-resolution images to make a good-looking print poster – make sure you generate images that are at least 300 dpi (vector graphics can scale up without loss of resolution, so keep your graphs and diagrams as vectors if you can). High-resolution image files can be large and will make a program like PowerPoint struggle on some computers. On a digital poster, your image resolution can be as low as 72 dpi, which means your files will be smaller and easier to handle.

Be especially careful how you treat your hero image. Don't put it at an angle to make it more obvious and never run text over the image unless you know how to handle opacity levels properly: the contrast between foreground and background needs to be correctly balanced. If you don't know what we mean by that previous sentence, just keep your text and images separate!

Remember that if you don't own the copyright in an image, you need to seek permission. Refer to the section on IP at the back of the book for how to do this. Be careful of people who claim that a poster constitutes 'fair use' of an image: this reading of copyright law reflects a pre-internet/social media understanding of the world.

Further reading

We've noticed that many people experience problems when they take images that are designed to be read in a journal article and blow them up bigger for the poster. Scaling up can reveal lots of problems and digital posters offer a range of animation possibilities that can bring your data to life. Luckily, there are a growing number of excellent books on visualising data – a result of the popularity of data visualisations on the internet. The classic of the genre is Edward Tufte's 'The Visual Display of Quantitative Information'[1]; a bit dated now (it was from the pre- high speed internet era), but the basic principles of truthfulness (and beauty) in data representation are timeless. If you want quite a prescriptive guide that won't steer you wrong,

'The Wall Street Journal Guide to Information Graphics' by Dona M. Wong is a simple guide to representing data accurately and well, written for journalists but approachable for anyone. For inspiration and ideas for truly next level data visualisation, we recommend 'Knowledge is beautiful'[2] by David McCandless. This book shows you how findings in any discipline, from history to physics, can benefit from thoughtful graphical treatments.

Notes on remote mode

- Fully online or hybrid conferences are probably here to stay. Digital posters are sometimes part of a conference format, usually displayed on a webpage, gallery style. The opportunity to use posters as a conversation starter is underexplored in virtual conferences – we hope this will change in years to come.
- Digital posters are still a great way to get your research in front of people. Even better, they can have a longer life than just the conference. Consider making your digital poster into a YouTube video, which can be shared on a large range of social media platforms.
- When your work is out there on the internet, you can't control where it will end up and what trouble it may cause. Read our section about IP at the back of the book if you do plan to distribute your poster outside of the conference setting.
- Be careful of using images from other people without permission (even if you alter them) and remember that diagrams you included in published papers are now technically owned by the journal, if you signed this right away. There is a difference between copyright (the right to distribute) and moral

rights (the right to be recognised as an author). If you have signed a copyright agreement, you'll need to seek permission to use previously published text and images, even if you created them yourself.

Notes

1   Edward R. Tufte, *The visual display of quantitative information*, Cheshire, CT: Graphics Press, 2001.
2   David McCandless, *Knowledge is beautiful: Impossible ideas, invisible patterns, hidden connections – Visualized*, San Francisco, CA: Harper Design, 2014.

8 Basic 20-minute conference talks

TL;DR

- Keep to time. Don't be the person who uses up other people's speaking slots at conferences or meetings. This will make you look like an amateur and will not make you any friends.
- Talk about what's new. Don't spend most of your presentation on background; write a script that devotes at least half the time to explaining your original contribution.
- Tell a story. There should be a clear structure that people can follow, but you can include techniques that increase tension and make your story more interesting.

In a nutshell

The 20-minute conference talk is the mainstay of your academic communication toolkit. The 20-minute talk format is so ubiquitous it's often treated as the only type of public talk academics give. Not true, as we will show you, but we like to think of the 20-minuter as the little black dress of academic presentations: an essential wardrobe item that can be made to fit many occasions. This chapter is a bit longer than others as

DOI: 10.4324/9781003197713-10

there are key skills here that can be adapted to other purposes, like lecturing and pitching for money.

The perfect 20-minuter should give people the basic 'what, why and how' of your research project, as well as the 'what next', without being boring or running over time. Given that most people can only say between 120 and 160 words a minute, getting all of this content in 20 minutes without talking superfast can be a challenge. Your aim is to be able to deliver a 20-minuter without sweating, shaking or stuttering. Getting good at the format can take a while, so go easy on yourself; there's a lot to learn.

The 20-minuter is most commonly found at conferences. Conference organisers often arrange the individual talks from each researcher into 90-minute sessions between breaks for food and conversation. Organisers try to group the talks in meaningful clusters of related papers to encourage people to come to the whole session. Each presenter is given a notional 30-minute slot within the session. It's conventional to talk for 20 minutes and leave around 10 minutes for questions, but you can talk the entire time. However, keeping to time and allowing space for questions sends a professional signal that you know the game and how it's played. The sure sign of the conference newbie is someone who gets to the end of 30 minutes and looks surprised that they are being asked to stop.

There's an important reason why you will be kept to time in a well-run conference. People like to move around between talks in each of the sessions, so organisers like all the talks to start and stop at the same time to allow for this movement. Usually someone in the room is tasked with keeping the session to time. It is considered deeply unprofessional to eat into a colleague's time, so it is critical to make sure your presentation is the right length. The 20-minuter is like an individual academic signature – everyone develops their own rhythm and style, but we recommend you take notes on people who do it well and copy their techniques.

How to prepare

Don't underestimate how much time it can take to prepare a good 20-minute presentation. We estimate it takes about 1 hour of preparation for each minute of the talk. Therefore, you should allow at least 20 hours to prepare a 20-minute talk from scratch. We've found this formula is good for predicting a worst-case scenario: as you get more familiar and comfortable with a topic, your preparation will take less time.

The best way to ensure you keep to time is to create a script – we'll have more to say on the content of the script below, but let's start with length. The number of words you include in your script will depend on your talking speed, but start with assuming you can say 120 words a minute. Write a script of at least 2,400 words for a 20-minute presentation and then time yourself reading it. Even better, record yourself reading it, which gives you an idea of your pacing (whether you are speaking too fast or too slow) as well as the length. Once you know your comfortable talking speed, you can make all your 20-minute scripts the same length.

Need to do a longer or shorter talk than 20 minutes? Simply divide 20 minutes by the number of words in your script to find out your own personal words-per-minute rate and apply accordingly. Follow this method and you will always give a precisely timed talk – trust us, this skill is rare enough that it impresses everyone.

The script is the basis of your performance. You can either read the script out, word by word, or distil it into talking points you can improvise around. The second strategy is riskier, and we only recommend it when you are confident with the material and prepared to practise a lot.

There are two options for building the script concept:

1   Design it as an oral piece from the start.
2   Read from a paper you have written, either in part or in full.

The approach you choose will depend on the norms in your discipline, personal preference and the nature of the story you are trying to tell.

If you are conceiving the talk as an oral piece, not a version of an academic paper, start by writing a script outline. The outline will include what each section of the talk will be about and how long it will be, as a kind of recipe outline. See the example below.

So you're graduating your PhD in a pandemic: what's next?

- Discuss the problem with the academic workforce before COVID and where PhD graduates find work (2 minutes)
- Describe the PostAc algorithm, and show some results and the platform screenshots (3 minutes)
- Show what is happening to the job market now compared to the past (3 minutes)
- Talk about the 'slow-burning crisis' of COVID and what it means for the future (2 minutes)
- Offer five suggestions for people to take charge of their post-PhD job search (2 minutes each for 10 minutes)

Use your outline to write your initial 2,400-word script in as close to 'everyday language' as you can manage. Use this script to make dot points if you feel confident enough to deliver that way. We have some more notes on different kinds of structures you can use to outline your talk later in the chapter.

Reading out an academic paper is the norm in some disciplines (looking at you, Philosophy, English and History). What you are really presenting in this case is a draft version of an academic paper with the intention of eventually publishing a finished version in a journal or book. The advantage of reading out a draft paper is to seek feedback from peers. This kind of talk is more common in the humanities because research outcomes are best expressed as arguments or insights rather than tables of data and findings of experiments. The words *are* the data in a way, so the dependence on an academic paper is understandable to make sure the argument is clearly communicated.

Although reading out a paper is the convention in some fields, it doesn't mean you should write a standard academic-sounding paper and just read it out. Written English is very different from spoken English. In fact, they have diverged so much they are now almost different dialects. Aim to write your draft paper 'academically', but in a way that is a bit easier on the listener. Here are some strategies:

- Use as few words as possible. Look for waste words like 'that', which tend to make sentences very long. Refer to good books on writing, such as *The Writer's Diet* by Helen Sword or the book Inger wrote with Katherine Firth and Shaun Lehmann, *How to Fix Your Academic Writing Trouble*, for ideas on slimming down your sentences.
- Generate a handout with the important wording on it – you may want to work your way through a handout rather than using slides. Or distil your handout onto a series of slides with a short amount of text on each one.
- Pay attention to your verbs. Lots of nominalised verbs (where verbs are turned into nouns) are difficult for listeners

to process. Words like 'argumentation' or 'implementation' are a mouthful and hard on the ear. Try writing a script with straight verbs like 'argue' and 'implement'.

* Cut down on left-branching syntax, where you have a lot of words before the key subject–verb–object structure in the sentence. Academic writing often features left-branching syntax; spoken language tends to have right-branching syntax, where the subject–verb–object appears early in the sentence and the extra detail follows. Read out the sentences below and you will notice the difference between left- and right-branching syntax:

> *Darwin studied finches.* (Simple subject–verb–object formation)
>
> *As part of his work on the* Beagle, *Darwin studied finches.* (Left-branching syntax)
>
> *Darwin studied finches as part of his work on the* Beagle. (Right-branching syntax)

How to be good at it

At its heart, the 20-minuter is a bit of academic storytelling. Your basic story has a beginning, a middle and an end so that people get a sense of progression and closure. Good stories feature some kind of change or journey. A great story generates a call to action: something the audience should think about or do differently. There are some simple story structures that you can take off the shelf and adapt to purpose. These structures can give your 20-minuter some storytelling punch and a through line that people can follow.

Let's look at two ready-made structures: Randy Olson's 'And, But, Therefore' (ABT) formula and Nancy Duarte's shape formula.

'And, But, Therefore' (ABT)

In his book *Houston, We Have a Narrative*, Randy Olson takes his lead from Hollywood screenwriters to help academics tell more compelling research stories. His ABT template is a simple sentence skeleton that helps you develop more tension in your talk. Olson points out that the word 'and' adds tension and the word 'but' changes the 'direction of the conversation'. The word 'therefore' sums up the *problem* you are trying to address. Generating an ABT statement creates a spine for your story that can shape your talk (or paper).

Let's look at some examples from Inger's research work:

Architecture teachers resist putting classes online **AND** claim that the classroom experience is central to learning to design **BUT** it's hard to resist management pressure to put classes online without evidence about what is unique about the classroom experience **THEREFORE** I studied what is unique about the classroom setting: hand gestures.

PhD graduates have a lot of amazing skills **AND** many would like to leave academia because there are not enough jobs **BUT** graduates report difficulty in identifying career paths in industry **THEREFORE** we designed a machine-learning algorithm to read job advertisements and show them all the possibilities.

PhD students often complain **AND** supervisors think this is a sign of a 'sick' research culture **BUT** academics have completely failed to understand the nature of these conversations and what they really achieve in practice **THEREFORE** we need to look more closely at the structure of this kind of 'troubles talk'.

For more detail about ABT, you can read *Houston, We Have a Narrative*, but for a better text on how to put it into practice, refer to Randy Olson's practical handbook *The Narrative Gym: Introducing the ABT Framework for Messaging and Communication.*

Story shape

Nancy Duarte's basic story shape draws on the 'hero' narrative developed in Joseph Campbell's work on the hero's journey. A great story, Duarte claims, is about transformation, and she suggests the best way to communicate this is to oscillate between 'what is' (the current problematic situation) and 'what could be' (the imagined future state). One way to action the Duarte shape is to use six different-coloured Post-it notes for the 'what is' and the 'what could be':

- **Post-it 1** summarises the existing problem.
- **Post-it 2** outlines the benefits (to the discipline or to stakeholders) of solving it.
- **Post-it 3** summarises what other people have done to investigate this research problem.
- **Post-it 4** outlines what you are planning to do differently.
- **Post-its 5 and 6** talk about the impact or outcomes of the research or, as Duarte puts it, 'the new bliss' with your research completed. Post-it 5 is a brief outline of the findings of your research, and Post-it 6 is how this knowledge changes the world (or your discipline) in some way.

Figure 8.1 shows how this approach can be used to summarise one of Inger's research projects.

There's too many PhD graduates and not enough academic jobs! It's hard to find a job 'outside' as not many employers ask for a PhD ... most of the job market is effectively hidden.

We need to expose the hidden job market so non-academic employers can better recognise their desire for graduates with research skills – and support grads.

Current research relies on retrospective self-report. If we ask employers, they say they don't need such 'highly educated' people, but their job ads suggest otherwise.

What is happening now and why is it a problem?

What becomes possible if this research is done?

How have other people researched this problem?

We taught a machine to 'read' job ads using ML/NLP. Finding the research-intensive job ads can reveal the size and extent of the hidden market.

We found there were 12 times more PhD-shaped jobs as graduates in 2017. There are not 'too many' PhDs – there are too few. We should be training more!

We can use these insights to transform employer acceptance and get more graduates into industry – and maybe to transform the PhD itself ...

How are you planning on researching the problem?

What does success in your research look like?

What is the long (or short term) impact of the research?

Figure 8.1 A story shape in practice.

Abstracts and titles

One last tip. The perfect 20-minute starts with the germ of an idea. This will usually be captured in the abstract you submit to get a chance to talk at the conference in the first place. An abstract is a short (around 400-word) piece of text that lays out the basic content of the talk. There are formulas for writing abstracts, which we won't labour over here. If you're interested,

Inger has written about this before in *How to Fix Your Academic Writing Trouble*, her book with Katherine Firth and Shaun Lehmann.

Many people say the purpose of the abstract is to tell people what to expect in the talk; we would say the purpose of the abstract is to *sell the talk and convince as many people to come as possible*. And this begins with a killer title.

Focusing on the title might seem a bit like we are emphasising the sizzle and not the sausage, but we believe that all researchers need feedback to fully develop their ideas. Conferences have become increasingly crowded over the years. Universities have made conference talks one of the many 'performance metrics' that measure the productivity of their academic staff. Conferences are usually run by small scholarly organisations who rely on the injection of attendance fees to finance year-on-year operations, so they will be keen to give as many people the chance to talk as possible. As a result, you are likely to be competing with lots of other talks and established speakers.

For new researchers, packed conference schedules are a problem on several levels. Early-career researchers tend to be given the shitty time slots: the morning after the conference dinner or the last session before everyone rushes off to catch their flight. You have to make a title that will convince people to get out of bed early or stay for the last session, rather than hitting the airport lounge for a free chardonnay. Your killer title has to make the person reading the schedule genuinely *want* to come and see you talk.

We have just one piece of advice about titles: be brave. Don't just describe what is in the talk; think about *why* the audience wants to be there and centre the title around that call to action.

- Boring: 'An analysis of the COVID-19 pandemic on the demand for research skills from non-academic employers'

- Better: 'So you're graduating in a pandemic. What's next?'
- Boring: 'The importance of research ethics to researchers'
- Better: 'Tragic research mistakes and how to avoid them'

Further reading

The 20-minute conference presentation is the most well-documented type of talk in academia; any book on presenting in academia will have decent coverage and offer tips. Therefore, we want to encourage you to look beyond the academic 'how to' genre and look at how pros in other areas of professional life engage and delight their audiences. We love *Resonate*[1] by Nancy Duarte. We already introduced you to Duarte's story shape in this chapter and encourage you to read more of her ideas and think about how you can apply them in practice. In a similar vein, *Presentation Zen*[2] by Garr Reynolds offers practical scaffolding for structuring engaging and memorable presentations.

Notes about remote mode

- The exhortation to make sure you observe the time constraints are even more important for remote conferences, where people might be tuning in from all over the world.
- Remote conferencing is great, but it does require a good internet connection, so consider putting more text on each slide than you normally would, to help people if the sound cuts in and out.
- Presenting remotely might provide you with the option to film your talk, then participate in the comments and answer questions as it plays.

- You can take advantage of conference software to film your live talk for the purposes of reviewing your performance or to create content for social media – see Chapter 15 on making short videos for ideas. These clips can be useful additions to your CV and helpful to send to people who would like a summary of your current research.

Notes

1 Nancy Duarte, *Resonate: Present visual stories that transform audiences*, New York: Wiley, 2013.
2 Garr Reynolds, *Presentation Zen: Simple ideas on presentation design and delivery (voices that matter)*, Indianapolis, IN: New Riders, 2019.

9 Keynotes and plenary talks

TL;DR

- A keynoter delivers the intellectual entertainment that opens or closes a big event. Speakers with good public profiles are often strategically chosen to make sure people turn up on time and stay right to the end.
- A keynote sets the tone of the event, while a plenary reflects on what has happened at the conference.
- In a keynote or plenary, engage people in some big-picture thinking about your discipline or practice, or key problems in the field.
- Make your talk relevant to everyone in the audience. Now is *not* the time for very detailed research findings that will only really interest a few. Give an overview of your own work in the field – focus less on detail and more on the connections between each project and how they contribute to knowledge.
- As well as talking about your own work, you can reference broader work in the field. This allows you to sketch out the current state of play in a problem, field or discipline.
- Some conference organisers want you to answer questions; others will give you the option to skip them. Make sure you have this discussion ahead of time so you can plan the appropriate amount of content.

DOI: 10.4324/9781003197713-11

- Have good visuals – including you. People often photograph keynote and plenary speakers in front of their slides. Make sure you brush your hair!

In a nutshell

In music, a *keynote* is the note on which a key is based; in practice, a keynote is used to help musicians work together; for example, the leader of a barbershop quartet often sounds the keynote before the rest of the troupe start to sing. So the keynoter of a conference 'sets the tone' for the rest of the meeting.

In a conference, there will often be several keynotes that are meant to set the tone for the rest of the academic conference to come. No other speakers will be scheduled at the same time, so this is a chance for the whole conference audience to gather in one place. The keynote speech is usually on a topic that will be of interest to everyone in the conference, related to the theme of the conference or a just an overview of the speaker's own contribution to the field. Keynotes are often used in conference advertising to convince people to come. You will only be asked to do a keynote if you have a high profile.

A plenary address closes a conference. The last day of a conference is sometimes sparsely attended as people head off to catch planes home. Conference organisers would like people to stay, which is why they tend to organise a plenary talk right at the end. The word *plenary* comes from the Latin term *plenarius*, meaning 'complete'. In an academic conference setting, the plenary is the 'last word' of the meeting. A plenary talk is expected to reflect the theme of the conference and will often incorporate something of the discussions that have taken place. Being asked to be a plenary speaker is quite an honour because the conference organisers try to find someone sufficiently high profile to encourage people to stay. Sometimes the plenary talker will be even more famous than the keynote, so if you are invited to give one, consider it an honour.

In summary, keynotes and plenaries are intellectual entertainment, and speakers are invited to attract people to the conference. We write this chapter because we are optimistic: if you are the kind of person who picks this book up and takes it seriously, it's likely that you will go on to be the sort of person who is invited to be a keynote speaker.

How to prepare

The keynote is more about star power than it is about really being a thought leader, and Inger says this with authority as she has done more than 20 of them. Most researchers in Inger's field would say she has interesting ideas and likes to do cutting-edge work, but they probably would not describe her as the most eminent thinker in her field. However, conference organisers know she has a following on social media, which will give the conference free publicity and (importantly) she is known in her field for putting on a 'good show'. By 'good show' we mean she will be thoughtful and interesting, but not too intellectually taxing.

The format for these talks is usually a bit longer – up to an hour in some cases. Being first to speak at a conference is a privilege, but it also carries responsibilities. No one else can start talking until you stop, so going over time is a definite no-no. Likewise, a plenary speech must be exquisitely timed so that people can take the last plane or train, or liberate their car from the parking garage before 6 pm. You are being invited because you are expected to be a consummate performer – and that also means knowing when it's time to shut up. People who are organising the conference are not going to stop you talking, so the onus is on you to be a professional. You will be rewarded by looks of relief and thanks from the organisers who do not have to instruct the caterers to try to keep the tea and coffee urns warm.

There are a couple of ways to approach putting on a good show. Here are some ideas.

- Try to focus in on a problem everyone has. This can be a problem of practice or the discipline itself, or a method. You don't have to solve the problem; you can just describe it really well and point out that someone should do something about it. This gives people at the conference some ideas to chat about at the tea table later.
- You can talk about cutting-edge work in your field and use the opportunity to boost the work of emerging scholars, or scholars who have been ignored. You might even dig out and dust off a thinker from 100 years ago and show how they were ahead of their time.
- You can be deliberately provocative and even a bit wacky. Remember, the real purpose of the keynote is to entertain, so some of the stricter rules about observing academic decorum are suspended. In one of Inger's first keynotes, she compared writing a PhD to a romance novel and used this as the spine for her talk (and an excuse to show a whole lot of lurid covers). People still talk about that one. Another time she did a plenary using *The Lord of the Rings* as a narrative arc. Simon once left a room full of Singaporean scientists reeling after his keynote on good science communication presented as 'dating advice for scientists', with special reference to all the medical professionals in *The Simpsons*. We've seen people riff on *Star Wars*, show a play-by-play from *World of Warcraft* or do a taxonomy of rubbish bins. They are the keynotes we remember. The serious ones? Nup – forgotten.
- If you are an eminent thinker with a long history of research behind you, you can treat the keynote as a kind of 'greatest hits' party. Take a whole lot of your research highlights and

make a kind of showreel. This will be boring if it's just an endless parade of 'look how great I am', so find a story. What ties all this work together? What is the overall narrative? If you are a detective, what is the crime you are solving? One memorable talk that Inger saw was an eminent scholar talking about all the research that went nowhere was unfunded or was dismissed. This was told in the form of a 'rags-to-riches' tale that was both riveting and relatable.

How to be good at it

While many of the tips we gave you in Chapter 8 on the 20-minute conference talk apply to a keynote or plenary, we recommend thinking a bit more carefully about content and tone of delivery. Here are some tips for keynotes.

- Don't give a detailed, serious talk about a bit of research in progress for a keynote. Like the pop stars who insist on only playing songs from their new albums, a sure way to disappoint a keynote audience is to do a narrow, focused talk on just the new stuff.
- Don't get on a rant about how everything was better in the old days: we've both been to a few of these, and they are super uncomfortable for the audience.
- Your job is not to solve the problem definitively or offer solutions: you are there to get people engaged in big-picture thinking. Raise questions for the audience to think about during the talk and at the end so that you give people conversational fodder for the tea break.

The plenary talk at the end of a conference is, in our experience, a harder thing to do than a keynote. Here are some tips for making a great plenary talk:

- It's OK to decide on the theme of the talk in advance and prepare a provisional script, but since you have 'the last word' you should not finalise the script until you have attended at least some of the conference.
- You'll be expected to try to tie the plenary talk into the themes or main concerns of conference. This means you should have spent at least some time absorbing what has gone on during the conference.
- You'll be more memorable if you tie the themes to specific examples. As you attend the conference, carry a notebook and jot down your observations on what seem to be hot topics of the meeting. What are people worried about?
- Give yourself time to pull the talk together: weaving the observations and notes into a prepared talk will take some time. And give yourself a bit of time to practise. Even just reading it out once or twice will get the 'feel' of the talk in your mouth and make the delivery smoother.

Since you are not expected to answer questions if you don't want to, it's good to plan the question time as a kind of bump space if you go over or under time. While many people are intimidated by famous people and won't ask a question, there are plenty of people who will, and the questions will often be very open ended. If you know your subject area well (which we will assume you do, because *keynote*), this is an invitation to just pontificate to your heart's content.

The crowd at a keynote or plenary is much bigger than for an ordinary talk, so your organisers will probably have to marshal microphones around a room. Big conferences tend to have tech support crews, so make sure you talk to them before you start so you are aware of the tech constraints. For example, if you are using a fixed microphone, ask where you need to stand for best sound quality; if there's a wireless mic, check how far you can walk from the microphone receiver. Check what lighting arrangements there are, particularly if the session is being filmed.

Further reading

It's even more important to look beyond academia for advice on how to make your keynote engaging, memorable and impactful. A classic of the business presentation genre is 'The presentation secrets of Steve Jobs' by Carmine Gallo. Steve Jobs, the founder of Apple, was the keynoter's keynoter: he redefined the business presentation in the 1990s and early 2000s. Despite being from a tech company, Jobs didn't rely on slides to give a great performance; the book unpacks how to structure a talk from start to finish: not the only way to do it of course, but full of useful information. When you're asked to keynote, you are probably already experiencing some minor form of academic fame. For a fun read on the pleasures and perils of public speaking fame, as well as some top practical tips for succeeding in different settings, we recommend *Confessions of a Public Speaker*[1] by Scott Berkun. While we are here, we want to point out that the conventional 'style' and expectations of public speaking have mostly been set by men. We are interested to see the emergence of books by and for women and can recommend *How to Own the Room*[2] by Viv Groskop, which also has great advice on conquering nerves and projecting confidence.

Notes on remote mode

- Remote conference keynotes are similar to the 20-minute conference talk in arrangement, but the audience will be expecting more of you, so learning to perform well to camera is critical.

- Often these talks are given in 'broadcast mode', where you will not even see people, Brady Bunch style, on the screen. The lack of feedback from the audience can make your performance pretty lacklustre unless you take extra steps to emote at the camera. Try putting a picture of someone's face in front of you and pretend they are listening – or have someone in the room with you, sitting behind the monitor.
- Sometimes, due to budget or time constraints, you will have to give your keynote remotely to a room full of people. Be aware that you are then a giant talking head and every pimple, blemish or piece of spinach between your teeth will be visible to everyone. It's hard to give a talk as a disembodied head, as you can't gauge the reception of the talk – is everyone bored? Or is it static that makes people look like they are shifting in their seats? If possible, ask the organisers to aim the camera at a couple of people in the first row so that you can get a better read on the audience.

Notes

1   Scott Berkun, *Confessions of a public speaker*, Sebastopol, CA: O'Reilly Media, 2009.
2   Viv Groskop, *How to own the room: Women and the art of brilliant speaking*, London: Transworld Digital, 2018.

10 Pitching for money

TL;DR

- You don't ask, you don't get! The squeaky wheel gets the grease. These clichés are, unfortunately, true. Keep talking to everyone about your research and why it's important. Don't be afraid to go way up the management chain to ask for help.
- Go to every workshop and briefing that has a hint of money attached to it: you find out so much more from people than from websites about what really counts in applying for internal research money.
- Keep management in the loop so they remember you and your research aims when there is largess to distribute!
- Universities are full of 'hidden' money and resources. Ask first for non-monetary support. It's important to success and often much easier to get. Leverage your networks to find out what you can ask for – and remember the university can help you access social networks in other departments and organisations.

In a nutshell

Sometimes an academic department can feel a bit like a large share house where one person is always upset about someone stealing

DOI: 10.4324/9781003197713-12

their yogurt out of the fridge. All departments have limited resources and academics have a very finely tuned fairness gland. They are pretty good at spotting when colleagues are getting more than their 'fair share' and will complain bitterly about it, usually over coffee on campus, or to their long-suffering spouses.

It's true that some people are very good at getting what they need from management – be it time away from teaching, a small pot of money to spend on equipment or graduate students to share the load. Those colleagues who are less good at putting their hand in management's pockets can be resentful of this 'special treatment', but the sad fact is that they probably have just not thought to ask. You can ask for money inside and outside of your university. If your university won't pay, consider talking to people in industry and government about your research aims and seeing if there is a mutually beneficial arrangement to be had. Consulting gigs can be a great way to develop new research tools and techniques on someone else's dime.

The art of asking for money without feeling embarrassed is within your grasp. Inger is fond of the saying 'If you don't ask, you don't get', but has noticed that some colleagues do not appreciate this kind of tough love. This might be because some people come from a 'guess' culture, not an 'ask' culture. In a guess culture, you expect people to just notice your needs and supply them to you; in an ask culture, you have to work harder to make your needs known. Academia is an ask culture: if you wait for people to guess what you need and give it to you, you will be waiting forever.

How to prepare

There are a number of ways to ask for help with your research inside your university. The easiest way is to make time to respond to internal funding opportunities, even if they are tiny bits of money to pay for conference fees and travel or a piece of equipment (it all looks good on the CV). Really this is just matter of keeping your eye on emails and applying. If you feel you fit some but not all of the criteria, it is sometimes worth just applying anyway. It's better to be told you are ineligible than to never apply in the first place. And you never know. There are often leftover funds or wiggle room for interpreting the rules if not enough people apply for a small pot of money. Inger once got an 'early-career researcher' grant this way, even though she was eight years past the end of her PhD.

Use your social network to increase your capacity to get any internal grants that come up. Notice what grants are being given to other people in your school. Always remember to send a congratulations email. Make a special effort to have coffees with these people or invite them out for drinks. Basically, you want to be on friendly terms with people who are successful at working the system. Casual conversation with people like this can be incredibly illuminating and open your mind to other resources that are available in your immediate environment.

Go to professional development and briefings

Put your hand up for all the extra professional development opportunities around grant writing and communications training. If you are still a PhD student while reading this, it's a no-brainer to go to Three Minute Thesis training. Most universities take part in this international competition, and there is no better way to learn how to craft compelling messages about your research. We've got some tips for the Three Minute Thesis in Chapter 4, but there is no substitute for the individual coaching that a face-to-face workshop can deliver. Many students do not attend training workshops, but they are an excellent place to meet people and learn insider tricks, even after you have finished your PhD (Inger notes that 15 per cent of people who come to her PhD training workshops are postdocs, so it's never too late to learn).

It's easy to be 'too busy' to attend professional development or briefings. Don't get stuck into thinking that 'effective work' equals an empty email inbox. Be strategic about how you use time. Prioritise events that look like they might be related to research money, even information sessions. You can learn so much from talking to the people who administer the grants. In our experience, grant administrators are full of little tips and tricks for writing applications. You'll kick yourself later if you miss a deadline or vital piece of information that would have resulted in a much-needed bucket of cash.

Tell managers what you're working on

Make sure management, especially your head of school or equivalent, knows what research you are doing. It's a good idea to book an appointment at least once a year to see your head of school to talk to them about your research plans and goals. If you feel particularly brave and passionate, also make time to talk to the dean in your area, the pro-vice-chancellor of research or similar. Inger even makes sure to see her vice-chancellor at least once every couple of years to update him on her research! The further up the management hierarchy you go, the more you encounter people who used to be researchers once but do very little of it now – and miss it. In our experience, people in high-up management roles are often happy to see and talk to working researchers, yet very few people approach them. If you do approach them, make sure you go in with a clear goal for the meeting – it might be just to let them know about blockages in the system, or opportunities they could be offering, rather than personal gain.

Send through published papers and other achievements to managers you are friendly with so they can see your successes, no matter how small. A lot of people shy away from this kind of signalling activity, but it's just part of being visible. As we've said repeatedly – people in academia are busy. Managers especially! But managers are often able to nominate people for opportunities and support. If you are in their face on a regular basis, they are likely to remember you when there is largess to be handed out.

Seek out 'third spaces'

Make it a habit to attend meetings and talks where people are using your kind of research. We're talking about 'third spaces' that are not academic and not industry but spaces where people are talking about common interests and concerns. These might be spaces generated by professional associations, for example the local chapter of your professional architects' network, a union of workers or a community group of concerned citizens. There are also meet-ups on a common interest topic in most cities, many of which are about technical tools or techniques. The purpose of hanging out in these spaces is twofold: to see what is troubling people (always a good starting point for research) and to make connections with people working in different sectors. Talk to these people about what you are doing – just making contact with people who are part of organisations with money to spend can be surprisingly fruitful and lucrative. Inger has scored two substantial pots of consulting money through connections made in these 'third spaces'.

How to be good at it

More than any other kind of communication activity, pitching for research is extremely audience focused. The person giving out money wants to know two main things.

1   What will the money be used for?
2   Can they trust you to achieve those aims?

If you can explain both, in sufficiently plain language, you are halfway to success already. Throw in some compelling metaphors and analogies (see Chapter 4 on lightning talks for more on this), and you might be surprised how easy it is to convince managers to open their institutional wallets. And find out what a 'reasonable ask' is in any given situation – there's very little point pitching a million-dollar research idea to someone who has an annual budget of ten grand.

Ask for in-kind support

We want to emphasise again that universities can support you in ways that don't directly involve money. In fact, the smart researchers often ask for 'in-kind' support and resources rather than money because these are easier for universities to supply. Here's a (non-exhaustive) list of support you can ask for.

- **Time release**. This doesn't have to be from teaching, which can cost money. You can ask for time release from things like committee work or a role in the school that carries an extra burden of work, like convening the first-year courses. You will be more successful in this kind of ask if you can demonstrate a history of being a 'good citizen' and doing your bit. As they say: you have to earn the right to ask for a favour.

- **Introductions**. Ask to meet other people doing similar work, inside or outside the university. Sometimes you will be offered a connection rather than money, but don't be annoyed – a solid relationship with another researcher who you can work with is better than a bunch of cash. One of Inger's most enduring research relationships was brokered by a government department who, instead of giving her a grant, put her in touch with a colleague within her own university! At the very least you will meet people of like mind who will be willing to have lunch with you.
- **Equipment**. You are more likely to succeed here if you can make the case that the tools will be beneficial to the whole department. Shared resources are one of the reasons universities exist in the first place. Given the shit fight that is your standard university website, asking is usually the way to find out if the tool or resource is already available!
- **Connections**. There is an invisible web of connections between all universities on the planet. Most are weak, but some universities have especially strong connections to others. You might be surprised by how these connections can be used to arrange all kinds of useful things, such as access to equipment, archives, libraries, fellowships, scholarships and partnership funding. Some of the connections are maintained by people in the centre of university management, while others are highly local affairs. You find out by being interested in what other people are getting and asking lots of questions, especially of people who have been on fieldwork or a sabbatical. Be forever curious about how your university is connected to others, and you shall find out how these connections can be leveraged.
- **Librarians**. There are a bunch of services libraries can provide, which are not immediately obvious until you ask for something special. Make an appointment to talk with the liaison librarian in your area, and you might be surprised

by how much help they can give you, especially with things like literature reviews and access to material not in your own library.

- **Specialist technical information and support**. The university is full of clever people who can help you who are not academics. Technical staff are often highly networked across campus because they work with people in every department and faculty. Their expertise can save you a whole lot of time and trouble if you know what to ask for – so get to know them. Be kind and thoughtful in your interactions with people who are not on standard academic contracts. We hear reports that some academics are arrogant and dismissive with these people – don't be that person and see what happens.
- **Special budgetary allowances**. You might be eligible for things like special stationery allowances if you ask. There are usually funds set aside in each department to provide over and above the standard level of support provided to most staff. Since this money is already earmarked and committed to a specific kind of task, you are not asking for money that has to come at the expense of something else in the budget.
- **Server space**. Increasingly academics are doing digital projects and using so-called 'Web 2.0' technologies that are hosted in cloud infrastructure. Before you go to an outside provider, check whether your institution can provide you access to server space, virtual or physical, to host your project.
- **Venue access**. Running a workshop, exhibition or product launch connected to your research can be considerably easier if you can get free or reduced-cost venue hire.
- **Connections to 'third spaces'**. Inger's university has a special relationship with the Canberra Innovation Network (CBRIN), which provides an amazing array of support, training and even desks for people doing research commercialisation. This is an example of a third space that is

government funded but serves as a bridge between the university and other entities. The people you meet in third spaces are extremely networked: it's their whole job. Every now and then, someone from CBRIN will take Inger out for coffee and offer advice or a new connection because they know what she is trying to achieve in her research. If you had to put a monetary value on this service, it would be in the tens of thousands of dollars.

Show the value of your proposal

Make sure, when you ask for anything over and above the basic allowances to academics – even if it's non-monetary support, that you are ready to make the value proposition for the university's investment clear. Inger recently went to see a high-up manager to ask for time release to support her PostAc research commercialisation. She thought carefully about it from his point of view and put the following points on a slide.

Income: Potential revenue from Australia and New Zealand is respectable, but potential global revenue is up to 10 times more. It's probably possible to do this project without VC investment, enabling more profit to be used for further R&D here in Canberra.

A quick win: ANU has a target of 10 start-ups within the next 5 years. We are closer than most projects on the runway and already have paying customers, demonstrating market demand. If ANU gives us

---

enhanced support for the next 18 months, they get more equity in spin-out and a lifetime licence to use.

Showcases the uniqueness of ANU: First spin-out of a cross-disciplinary project involving 'both sides of the creek' and CSIRO. ANU brand associated with national prosperity: helping Australian industry find the talent they need to innovate and grow.

Gender equality: This project has three female founders. Our success will put us in the position to mentor and encourage other women at ANU, who currently do not take part in commercialisation at the same rate as men.

Future innovation: The team behind the product are talented and capable – now they are also experienced at development and commercialisation of new products. We have a history of working with talented students who could be drawn into this start-up. What more can we do?

The manager stopped her halfway through and said, 'I'm convinced. What can I do to help?'

You too may end up commercialising your research; this way of making impact is becoming more common as governments provide incentives to drive innovation out of the university sector. Part of the commercialisation journey is to pitch your ideas to investors, which is not dissimilar to the kind of pitches you see on shows like *Dragons' Den*. There is not room here to do justice to the skills you need to pitch for money outside the university, but we recommend you look carefully at Chapter 4 on lightning talks for some tips that translate into these more commercial settings.

Further reading

There's a growing literature on pitching in academia – we all need money! For a great starter book, we recommend *The Research Impact Handbook*[1] by Mark Reed which is full of useful case studies (we also enjoyed his book *The Productive Researcher*[2] which has tips on how to create the kind of work that requires skills in pitching in the first place). Again, looking outside academia is a good idea: most of the popular business literature is about convincing people to hand over money. To help her sell the PostAc platform (www.postac.com), Inger turned to *Pitch Anything*[3] by Oren Klaff. Klaff claims his method is built on brain science, all Inger knows is that it definitely works as it's helped her land about seven deals, and counting…

Notes on remote mode

- There's no doubt that the kind of free-form socialising and detective work that we advocate in this chapter can be much harder online. Third spaces, like CBRIN in Canberra, still do still run meet-ups and presentations over Zoom, but interaction is mostly in chat and kind of stilted. Still, it's worth going just to see who is doing what so you can make offline meetings with interesting people.
- Universities are still running professional workshops online, but this format largely loses the social dimension, making them much less effective spaces for forging long-term relationships. Again, just showing your face is a good idea and will give you intel about who is doing what to follow up on separately.
- You will have to be much more proactive in building a social network when you have to do it from home. Use LinkedIn

to search for interesting people to talk to, and reach out for an online meeting via email. See Chapter 3 on writing emails about your research for some tips.

- Having some of the useful one-on-one conversations, especially with support staff, is to some extent easier via technology. It's much easier to make a meeting via Zoom or Teams than to travel to an office on campus or meet in a café.
- If you have restricted mobility for any reason, social media platforms like Twitter are an excellent source of intel on what you can ask for from your university or how to approach problems. Inger crowdsourced just about all the tips about non-monetary support via Twitter on Christmas Eve!

Notes

1   Mark S. Reed, *The research impact handbook*, Huntly: Fast Track Impact, 2018.
2   Mark S. Reed, *The productive researcher*, Huntly: Fast Track Impact, 2017.
3   Oren Klaff, *Pitch anything: An innovative method for presenting, persuading, and winning the deal*, New York: McGraw Hill, 2011.

11 Impromptu 'elevator pitches'

TL;DR

- Know what you want from the interaction before you start engaging – what does success look like?
- Say the most important thing first – and try to make it memorable and interesting.
- Don't be afraid to make it personal. The person in front of you will be captivated by your excitement and motivation to undertake the work.
- Powerful people might not appear to listen – this doesn't mean they have not heard what you said. Give them a way to follow up by having a business card handy.

In a nutshell

We all know the old story: an impoverished researcher looking to finance their next project steps into an elevator, and standing there with his chequebook in his hand and a smile on his face is Bill Gates. Mr Gates presses the button for the penthouse (naturally), which gives our hapless researcher the time it takes for the elevator to get to the top floor to impress Mr Gates and extract a few million in research funding.

DOI: 10.4324/9781003197713-13

Or so the story goes.

Whether it's a passing billionaire in a lift or just the new vice-chancellor pausing at your workstation on a whistle-stop tour of the faculty, time is definitely of the essence in this scenario. You only have a few seconds – at most a minute – to get your message across and to impress. So, what do you say?

Any good communicator knows how to think on their feet and shouldn't be fazed by any audience – no matter how well known or important they are. A good communicator is also primed and ready to trot out an impressive 30-second, 3-minute or 30-minute talk on their work at the drop of the proverbial hat. So, while your elevator pitch may well be unexpected, such an eventuality should never find you unprepared. Besides, you have practised all these skills in research meetings (read Chapter 2 if you need a refresher). Without even blinking, you will have all your facts marshalled in your head. If you read our chapter on talking about your research in social settings (Chapter 5), you will have a logline prepared as an opener. Ideally, you'll have a couple of fascinating facts and an anecdote or two at your fingertips. Like all good, engaged academics, you will know what is going on in the world – especially the news of the day – and be able to show how switched on and connected you are, enabling you to relate what you do to any current developments in the wider world. The key thing to remember here is that you need to tailor your delivery to the audience so you can get some kind of positive outcome. Let's look more closely at what that outcome might be.

How to prepare

Before you open your mouth, spend a second or two thinking: 'What do I want to get out of this interaction?'

Billionaires in lifts aside, every interaction can have a series of possible outcomes. The quicker your computer-like brain can process the options and alight on the most appropriate outcome for the situation, the more focused and more effective your elevator pitch will be. So, ask yourself: are you after funding or do you want to influence someone in power? Is there an opening in the department you have your eye on? Or do you feel your project has been overlooked and just needs a little leg-up in the promotional stakes? In the blink of an eye, you should be able to mentally complete the sentence: 'If the next three minutes goes well, I will …'

Essentially, what you are doing is setting the destination for the short journey you and your audience are about to go on together. Remember your audience in this situation will have very little time and very little attention to give you. We suggest the very first thing you say is what you want them to remember. Usually this will be a key finding – even better, a surprising one. Anything that you can get across to them after that will be a bonus.

Start with the most important thing

In journalism, people often talk of the 'inverted pyramid' structure, which is relevant in this situation. The inverted pyramid – with the big end up top, but narrowing down to a very fine point at the bottom – is predicated on the fact that your average newspaper or magazine reader is only ever skimming, their eyes darting across the pages looking for something to alight on and read. The reader is highly distractible, always looking for something more interesting, even as they read your article. So, the impact of what you say diminishes as the audience progresses through the piece and, one by one, drifts off elsewhere. Having started with a full house up top, by the time you are at the base of the structure, you might only be talking to 20 per cent of your readers.

As with newspaper readers, so it is with Elon Musk or the dean of the faculty in a corridor: important people are capable of leaving your beautifully crafted speech half-said and moving on to the next interesting person, if the mood takes them. If you say the most important thing at the start – the big end of the pyramid – you are sure to 'land' your message with the busy, important person even if you only have 10 seconds of their attention.

So, if you have cured an incurable disease or discovered a new planet or unearthed a hitherto unseen Shakespearean sonnet, that better be the very first thing you say to an important person. If they are in two minds whether to keep listening, your compelling opening statement may well tip the balance in your favour. Your goal is to use this first line to get them listening attentively, and even smiling and nodding. Or, if you've come across the great person on an off day when they really, really want to be left alone, at least you've told them what you've achieved. If they pass on the chance to hear more, you can tell yourself you gave it your best shot.

Add in the personal

Once your target is drawn in by your opening line and is reeling in shock, heart palpitating in excitement from your revelations, follow up by explaining *why* you undertook this research. This is contrary to everything you've been taught, we know, but it helps if you can make your research personal. This is where you briefly suspend the idea of 'getting the data out there' and put yourself in the picture – ideally front and centre. Essentially explain why you came to this area of study; talk about what your personal angle is. Not only will this help address the question of why a vast fortune in research dollars should be given to you, rather than anyone else in your field, but getting personal will probably help you overcome any nerves you might have and release the passion that drove you to your work in the first place.

We don't care if Jeff Bezos has spent a lifetime listening to people pitch at him: hearing an expert get excited – even emotional – about their work is one of the most convincing things an audience can hear. If you had a Eureka moment early on, this is the time to share it. And don't feel the need to mask it with academic talk – you can be quite conversational here. There's a great Three Minute Thesis competition example of an otherwise clinical and reserved scientist looking down a microscope and seeing something that no living being had ever seen before. 'It blew my mind' is all he can say, but the effect of those few words and the passion behind them had the hairs standing up on the backs of our necks.

After that, if you are lucky enough to get this far, offer any technical background you feel will help our itinerant billionaire understand your process and back up your credentials, and invite questions.

Assume the person is listening

If the busy person does not acknowledge what you said, don't assume they are not listening. Inger once had about 30 seconds to get the attention of a cabinet minister during a visit to Parliament House. She told him that he wasn't training enough PhD graduates, that he needed to train more and that she could prove it with numbers. He was so used to people saying there were too many PhD students that her first line hooked him in and enabled her to get a grand total of four more sentences out before he stopped paying attention and literally turned to the man standing next to her and started asking him a question. Inger went back to her office downhearted, convinced he hadn't heard a thing she said and harbouring some degree of feminist rage. But it seems that busy, public people are used to talking and listening at the same time. They also have staff hanging around with them, listening in. In this case, the minister included Inger's factoid in a speech the following month, complete with facts and figures she had made publicly available. As it turns out, her unusual fact had caught his attention enough that he asked one of his staff to follow up and put it in a speech. Mission accomplished! (Even if he was a rude bastard.)

How to be good at it

Thus far you've talked about you and your work – ideally in a very dynamic, impactful and quite personal way – but don't forget a conversation is a two-way process. Any act of communication, even if your audience does not speak, is tantamount to a conversation. So, what do you know about the person you are addressing?

Chances are, if your target is well known, important or higher up in your field, you probably know quite a bit about them. Use that knowledge to tailor your micro-talk to your audience. Ask yourself which part of your work might be of interest to them or, alternately, how you can present your work in a way that it appeals to their personal areas of interest. Your research is almost certainly wide in its remit. You will not have time to talk about all of it, and your audience probably doesn't need to hear all of it, even if they had the time. So home in on what is most relevant. Simon often describes this process as being a lot like mining – your research is like a huge, seemingly impenetrable rock face, but hidden in there are seams of gold or precious stones. A good communicator can quickly sum up which of these their audience is looking for and then offer it up to them in an accessible and engaging format.

As you finish speaking, always leave your audience with a little gem of information that will stay in their minds forever. Even if – as per the inverted pyramid – you're talking to a reduced crowd, it's important to try and make sure those interested souls have a lingering memory of you and your work. Indeed, the most important parts of any presentation, whether it be 2 minutes or 2 hours long, are the very first thing you say and the very last thing you say. The opening line is what journalists refer to as a 'hook' because it does just that – it hooks your audience and reels them in – and the last thing you say is like the very last chord of a symphony that rings in the air long after the orchestra has packed away their music stands and gone down the pub. Finish your elevator pitch with a line on what you hope to achieve. Is it going to be a game changer or reshape how we think about things? Don't hide your light away: a little bit of modesty is OK, but there's nothing wrong with being proud of what you do and showing how you are aiming for the stars.

Then, if we really are talking about a billionaire in a lift, you'd better make sure to hand over a business card, or mention an instantly memorable website, or at least suggest that you will follow up this little chat with Bill's 'people' in the next few days. Finally, a nice warm smile, some sort of gesture – a handshake, a small bow or the Thai *wai* (Simon's personal favourite) – and an offer to answer any questions they may have will round off the encounter nicely. If you can manage all this at the drop of a hat before the elevator doors open, the cheque, as they say, is in the mail.

Further reading

Again, the best preparation for presenting at short notice is to practise, practise, practise but many people just… don't. The on-your-feet-no-preparation pitch is really confronting and, at the same time, relatively easy to avoid – just don't open your mouth! The moment is gone and so are your opportunities. Building confidence is a job of work in itself, and some of these skills are better learned in therapy than from books. The self-help shelves are filled with these books, but given how many have frankly toxic 'just get over yourself' messages, we recommend sticking with the books by people who actually have some kind of scholarly background. Inger is a huge fan of Brené Brown's whole repertoire, which is aimed squarely at this problem. The best of her books for this kind of confidence building is probably *The Gifts of Imperfection*.[1]

Notes on remote mode

- Chance encounters are only possible if people are out and about, so the pandemic has drastically curtailed this aspect of research communication. You can still 'encounter' important people on social media – you can engineer this by tagging them into a conversation.
- On most social media platforms, the mention of a person's handle will enable them to have some degree of visibility of your comment. They can choose to respond to you, or amplify. They may even move the conversation to another channel like email if they are sufficiently interested. We know a few researchers who have succeeded landing crucial support this way.
- As in person, don't expect the busy, successful person to answer. At time of writing, Inger has more than 100,000 followers on social media and gets tagged into tweets all the time. If the person keeps their comment interesting and relevant, it's welcome contact.

- If you are concerned about your future reputation, don't tag a powerful person in just to criticise them. At least one academic we know has become a target of legal action for commenting on politicians' behaviour, so be careful (although Inger tagged the former Australian prime minister so many times on critical comments that she has thoroughly burned that particular bridge).
- Remember it's easy to become a pest on social media: if you have tagged someone a few times hoping to get their attention and they don't respond, cease and desist.

Note

1   Brené Brown, *The gifts of imperfection: Let go of who you think you're supposed to be and embrace who you are*, Center City, MN: Hazelden Publishing, 2010.

Part III

The wider world

You've successfully navigated your way through a PhD, or you are nearly finished. You've participated in some pitching and competitions inside your university. You have important findings, and people outside your university are starting to take an interest. All of a sudden you're a budding media star, with invitations to go on the TV and the radio – maybe even take to the stage to deliver a TED Talk. This is good news – except for the nerves you're feeling perhaps. You might be wondering now: how do you cope with this newfound fame and not embarrass yourself in public?

In this section of the book, we help you interface with 'real' media players such as journalists, take part in panels, make a documentary about your research and play around on social media. You don't have to wait until the end to dive into all this stuff, but it helps to have some substantial research findings to share first, so we put it right at the end. By the time you finish these chapters, you will be well and truly ready for your close up!

DOI: 10.4324/9781003197713-14

12 Being the 'good guest' on an invited panel

TL;DR

- When you're invited to a panel, you need to be able to play the role of 'good guest'. This performance starts when the invitation arrives. Communicate with the organisers early and often.
- Success on panels is much like success at dinner parties. Don't be the person who hogs all the attention – and be prepared to help the chair out in managing other people who do.
- Find out as much as you can about the other people you will be on the panel with. Being able to connect their work with yours enhances audience experience and shows you are a gracious participant.
- Just say yes to the microphone!

In a nutshell

Panel discussions are the mainstay of conferences and festivals and are hugely popular with audiences everywhere. Done well, they are a great way to promote lively debate, both on the stage and in the audience afterwards, making them great opportunities for you to shine on stage and make some very useful

DOI: 10.4324/9781003197713-15

connections. Done badly, of course, they can be like watching paint dry.

Just as when you write, you are writing *for your readers*, when you are a guest on a panel, you are taking part in the panel *for the audience*. They've turned up specially to see you and your co-panellists, and they may have even paid good money for the privilege. It's very flattering to be considered enough of an expert to sit on stage with other experts – sometimes, quite excitingly, even the leaders from your field – but you need to remember that you are only a part of that panel and that, certainly as far as the organisers and the audience are concerned, the success of the panel *as a whole* is what matters, not the individual guests. Obviously, you are also hoping to gain some benefit for yourself – possibly with book sales, exposure, connections, kudos, etc. – but put simply: a good panel is an exercise in teamwork.

When you speak on a panel at a conference or a festival, it's very important to remember you are giving what is essentially a performance. Your work is still the same. Your expertise is still the same. But you're not writing about it, you are taking part in what is tantamount to a small theatrical performance, with all that that entails. So, while what you are taking part in could well be quite an intimate conversation, you are doing it for the benefit of all the other people who are listening in. Physically this might mean things like facing your co-panellists three-quarters on so the audience can see your face, or sitting under hot stage lighting, or even having a slightly stilted conversation where you and your co-panellists all know exactly what you are referring to, but you need to spell it out for your less specialist audience.

How to prepare

While panels tend to consist of spontaneous, unrehearsed conversations, there is still a lot you can do in advance to prepare yourself to be a good panellist. Like they say in Scouting, you should always be prepared – and that means doing your homework.

Read the invitation carefully

Being a good guest starts when the invitation arrives in your inbox. In fact, everything you do from then on leading up to the moment you walk out onto the stage is as important as what you do and say once the spotlight is shining on you. Start by reading the invitation very carefully. If it's a well-written invitation, it should set out exactly what they want you to do and what they are offering you in return for your services. And, if it doesn't, you need to ask. Asking for more information shouldn't cause offence, and, if it does, that should give you pause for thought: is this an invitation you really want to accept?

Exercise a degree of caution with a generic invitation – you may well be invited as 'an esteemed guest', but does that mean captivating the opening-night crowd of 2,000 at the Town Hall or just giving a 15-minute talk to an equally small number of people and then helping stack chairs and do a little light sweeping afterwards?

Respond to the invitation

Good manners say you should reply to an invitation as soon as you receive it. Practicality says you might need a day or two to check your diary and wrangle any other conflicting commitments you may have, but if it is going to take any longer than that, you need to immediately tell the organisers. One thing that characterises a 'difficult' guest is someone who assumes event organisers are mind readers and know what their guests are thinking. And, if you do have to decline, no matter what the reason, be polite and gracious about it; you may well want to be invited back in subsequent years.

The details really need to be crystal clear right from the start. And that means on both sides. If the invitation says that they are a small community organisation with no budget who are relying on guests to make their own way to the venue, it would be unreasonable of you to get stroppy six months later and start demanding an airfare and five-star accommodation. Equally, if you are happy to do a panel but not a solo session, make that clear from the start.

When an event is transporting and accommodating you, possibly even giving you a fee, you are 'on their dime', as they say. Which means it's fairly bad form to sneak in extra appearances or other paid gigs for other organisations so you can make more money out of the trip. If this is a possibility, discuss it with your host organisation in terms of a potential joint venture or collaboration. Upfront and honest is always the best way.

Keep communicating

Good communication from the initial invitation through to the event itself is vital for both the organisers and the present-ers to get the most out of your participation. If you have any requirements – anything from dietary preferences through to needing a projector and screen on stage – these should be worked out as early on in the process as possible. Last-minute requests can be a real headache for organisers. Don't be the guest who decided he needed a tailor's dummy on stage the day before the festival, otherwise he couldn't possibly go on. Seriously!

Research the details

Find out as much as you can about the panel, your fellow speakers, the panel chair, the potential audience and even the overall event itself. You really don't want to be dealing with surprises on stage, and nothing endears you to an audience like referring to the previous year's keynote and the reverberations it sent through the community. Referring to a fellow panellist's work will show you to be intelligent and well informed, and will guarantee you will be treated with respect. And, if you are completely across your fellow panellists' work and the topic that has been set for the panel, you can pretty much anticipate where the discussion will go and be ready to address any issue that might arise.

You should also know the logistics inside out – when is the panel on, where is it to be held, how are you getting there; who's meeting you; and if there is a meeting point, on-site office or green room you should report to. Always be on time, preferably a little early; nothing makes an event organiser more nervous than a speaker who arrives literally minutes before they are due to go on. In fact, you should really plan to arrive early and make use of the green room or nearby café to relax and psych yourself up to do a good job. Rushing on stage out of breath is not a good look and probably means you're not going to perform at your best. If you have anything that needs to be stashed away while you are on stage, you'll want to deal with that nice and early too. Try not to be the panellist who brings their shopping on stage with them – it's not a great look and your ice cream will melt under the bright lights.

How to be good at it

Success as a member of a panel is a lot like success as a good dinner-party guest. You can say too much and dominate, but equally you can say too little and be a wallflower. There is definitely a Goldilocks setting here. The event's organisers are hoping for a panel where ideas are exchanged in a lively, even controversial, but ultimately civilised and mutually respectful manner. They want a panel where everyone gets a say, and no one is sidelined or left out. Theoretically, it is the chairperson's job to ensure this, but sometimes you can play an active role as a panellist. A perfect example would be a crime fiction panel Simon once witnessed where one of the panellists had come directly from a long lunch and decided to hold forth loudly and at great length. Unfortunately, the chair of the panel was unable to rein him in with the result that the most talented writer on the panel, who was also painfully shy, was in great danger of being steamrollered. Enter the perfect guest who orchestrated – there is no other word for what she did – the conversation so that our ebullient friend still felt he was the centre of attention, but the blushing wallflower was allowed to get many a wise word in edgeways.

Humour, or at least a good-humoured approach, goes a long way to making you come across as a likeable and, therefore, successful panel member. Even the most serious of topics can be discussed with moments of lightness; no audience member wants to wade through an hour or so of non-stop doom and gloom. So, lighten up a little, and if you want to channel your inner Stephen Fry or Hannah Gadsby, go for it! It helps to mentally rehearse some spontaneous remarks, as counter-intuitive as that sounds. Any good public speaker will have a little stash of clever, witty, funny one-liners and anecdotes that they are able to draw on and deliver in a fresh and spontaneous way again and again and ... well, you get the picture.

Just as good panellists can really help make a panel special, it only takes one rotten panellist to spoil the whole barrel. Event organisers all have horror stories about such guests. A classic but sadly not that rare story would be the one about the panellist who sent in a completely incorrect biography only to look up in horror when it was read out on stage and protest loudly about its inaccuracy. All in the name of attention seeking. Don't be that guest.

Don't hog the stage time. In an ideal world, every panellist should get roughly the same amount of airtime – obviously there will be a degree of tolerance and flexibility here, but if an hour-long event features four speakers and your 'brief' opening remarks are about to hit the 29-minute mark, you are not being fair to your fellow panel members.

And, if the venue says you need a microphone, assume you need a microphone. Don't, whatever you do, push the mic aside and declare confidently: 'I am sure everyone can hear me.' First, the sorts of guests who do that are invariably the quiet ones who can't be heard. Second, you have no idea what the microphone is there for: there are so many things that they can be used for other than amplification in the room you are in. Your session might be being recorded, it could be piped through to another room (an 'overflow' room for a sell-out session or when a 'cry baby' option is offered to parents of young kids) or it could be fed into a hearing-aid loop which might be meaningless to you on stage, but which can make the difference between an enjoyable discussion and a waste of time to audience members with hearing difficulties. Just use the microphone!

The keys to looking good in question time are preparation and the ability to think on your feet. Think about it: you know your topic, you have researched your fellow panellists' areas of expertise and you are well aware of any current developments in the field so it should almost be impossible for you to be surprised by a question. A good panellist anticipates every possible question and prepares appropriate answers in their head. There are, of course, a few tricks of the trade to make question time even more painless. The thoughtful 'That's a very interesting question…' or the repetition of the question out loud as though you are pondering the weight of it are just a couple of the delaying tactics you can use to think through an answer. And never forget you are part of a panel of experts – palming off a tricky question to another panellist with the flattering line 'This is very much your area of expertise, isn't it, Barry?' while you quickly think how you might answer will also buy you time.

While you are engaging in off-the-cuff conversation on stage, all the rules of printed and online publication apply. Essentially, announcing something in public pretty much counts as it is being 'published'. So – no divulging trade secrets or matters that are commercial in confidence; no slandering, libelling, general name calling or hair pulling; and definitely no claiming others' ideas as your own without some sort of nod to their creator. Just as you should always think before pressing <Print> or <Send>, you should always think before opening your mouth on stage.

Lastly, taking part in a panel discussion should be fun. Think about it: you get to talk about yourself, your work and your passion, and people sit there listening with rapt attention. How good is that? So don't be overawed by it. Just do your homework, turn up on time and enjoy yourself!

Notes on remote mode

- We find there is less interaction between panellists in online spaces as it is not as easy to co-ordinate talk, so while all the tips we give above are valid, you will need to follow the lead of the chair more than in a face-to-face setting.
- While universities tend to use similar technologies and even have syndicated logins for easier access, online technologies can vary greatly from organiser to organiser. Don't assume you know the technology if you've never used it. More than once, Inger has been unable to exit the 'green room' and been late as a result. If the organiser offers a practice session, we suggest you take it.

- Always make sure you have the mobile number of one of the organisers so you can check in if you are having trouble.
- Online public events can have large audiences – that's a lot of people looking at your dirty dishes if you have to present from the kitchen table. Unless you have one of those homes where everything is spotless all the time, use a virtual background. You might be given one by the organiser to brand the session anyway.
- If you do a lot of online presentations, it might be worth investing in a good microphone and even a backdrop cloth. You can use basic black as your backdrop, but a green cloth can assist your computer to patch in a virtual background without losing most of your hair!

Further reading

There are very few books that guide you on how to be a good panellist, which is why we included this chapter. You can, however, learn a lot from books for event organisers. These books help you see the problem of putting on events from the other side of the lectern, so to speak – a perspective that can help you better understand the role you are playing. The best one we've read is *The Art of Gathering*[1] by Priya Parker, which shares the secrets of what elevates ordinary events into extraordinary and memorable ones. For our money, this is one of the best books to read if you want your teaching to be amazing as well.

Note

1 Priya Parker, *The art of gathering, how we meet and why it matters*, London: Penguin Books, 2019.

13 The art of media interviews

TL;DR

- Anticipate what you are going to be asked so you are not surprised by journalists' questions.
- Journalists do not run interviews the way researchers do. Watch what you say as misunderstandings can be hard to retract.
- Find out why the journalist wanted to speak to you specifically. This can help you work out what they expect to get from you.
- Find out if you are going to be live or pre-recorded. Pre-recorded interviews can allow for more retakes if you stuff up. Journalists are generally reluctant to change a story once they have written it, so be careful to say what is on the record and what isn't.

In a nutshell

Media interviews are such a vast topic they could have been a book in their own right, but let's start with print. These days this is not just ink on paper but pixels on screens in all shapes and sizes too. While a print interview can be done face to face

DOI: 10.4324/9781003197713-16

over a coffee, increasingly journalists are so busy and over-worked they will interview you over the phone or by Zoom, Teams or some other online service. Occasionally you might even get the questions as an email to respond to in your own good time.

If you are meeting the journalist or seeing them on a screen, treat the occasion like any important meeting – dress to impress, turn up on time and in the right place and make sure you are ready to talk about the topic in question. With interviews like this they might record what you say, take notes, transcribe or summarise the interview later and then use that material in their story. This means you need to be crystal clear in everything you say. By the time the readers see the story, the information will already be second hand, with the journalist conveying your meaning on your behalf.

If you are talking on the radio or being recorded for a pod-cast, you need to know whether you will be talking to them from your home or whether the interview will take place in a studio. You might even find yourself in a closet; Inger has lit-erally asked guests on her podcasts to sit in closets as the small space and abundance of soft material makes for an excellent recording environment! The ABC has a mini studio known affectionately as the Tardis, which is essentially a cupboard with a microphone and a pair of headphones on a tiny desk. The Tardis is exactly what it sounds like except that, after a day of being beamed live to regional radio around the country, the room will feel even smaller on the inside than the cupboard it first looked like on the outside.

Before you go on radio, find out if you are talking live (no pressure, but what you say is what will go to air!) or if you are going to be pre-recorded for broadcast later (which means they can edit you and, if you really make a bad mistake, you can ask to do it again). A phone interview is the easiest – you can do it in bed in your pyjamas if you like, but the sound quality isn't always the best and, if the sound is particularly bad, you might find your interview cut short or even cancelled altogether.

As daunting as a studio can be, we'd suggest you take this option if you can as you will always end up sounding better. Make sure you do a small vocal warm-up (even if that's only getting a glass of water and clearing your throat) and be aware of good microphone technique. In a studio, the producer will tell you where to sit and how to close to be. After they sound check you in that position, don't move and keep your volume about the same. It won't make any difference to the audience, but eye contact with your host will make for a smoother, more intimate conversation. And be prepared for talkback if you are on live. Usually, the host will check if you're happy to take questions from the public, but don't act surprised if they suddenly spring it on you.

Commercial television interviews are a bit of a rarity these days, but the rise of YouTube, vodcasts and the like has more than filled the void this has created. The key in a TV interview – and this might sound obvious, but you'd surprised how many people need reminding of this – is that *you'll be seen*. So, you need to look your best. Cameras are more forgiving than they once were, but stay away from red if you can and avoid narrow stripes and small prints that do something called 'strobing' on camera. Chances are also high that someone will pin a small microphone on you, which means they will need somewhere to pin it. As Inger is fond of saying, the patriarchy invented recording equipment and assumes you will be wearing a suit and tie. A lapel is the best place for a mic so wear a jacket if you can – and avoid the sort of clunky jewellery, especially earrings, that plays havoc with the mic and infuriates the sound technician.

Try not to look at the camera unless they ask you to. Usually, the interviewer will position themselves just to the side of the camera so you will be looking slightly off camera. Just keep your eyes on the interviewer and have a conversation with them. And act natural. The more natural you act, the better you will look on camera. The interviewer may well do an exaggerated version of smiling and nodding to encourage you to keep talking, but don't be tempted to follow suit.

How to prepare

The real key to success when you talk to the media is preparation, which means anticipating anything and everything that could possibly be asked so nothing can take you by surprise.

As obvious as it sounds, make sure you know the sort of interview you are going to give: are we talking print, radio or TV, and is it online or in person, live or recorded? When you start out, you'll only be doing a small number of interviews and you'll almost certainly be doing them one at a time, so this question won't be hard. When you are more advanced in your career, or when you do something that makes you the centre of attention, it can be hard to get your head around the numerous interviews that will fill your diary. Essentially: be organised.

Always think about out how the interview came about: who suggested the journalist talk to you specifically? Was there a media release about your research or did the journalist find you because of something you posted on social media? The origin of the interview can imply very different types of questions. Thinking about what prompted your involvement will give you clues as to what the interviewer might want to know and the sort of story the interviewer is hoping to file. Trust us, even just this small amount of preparation can make a difference on the way things will play out on the day.

Then you should find out about the person is going to be talking to you. And you need more than just a name here – while we're not looking for a full background check, you should at least know what they normally write about, what the last story they had published was, whether they are a freelancer or on staff, that sort of thing. The best interviews tend to be a bit more of a conversation than a straight-out, one-sided interview so the more you know about the person you are going to be chatting to, the better that conversation will be. Plus, there's no better way to get a journalist on side than by opening with some flattering remarks about the last story they had published.

Ask for the questions if that's possible – most journalists will not provide them in advance, but it depends on the piece. If it's a documentary-style piece, it will be in the journalist's interest for you to be well prepared, but they may also spring questions on you.

You should always make sure the logistics are completely clear: where and when is the interview going to take place? Will it just be the interviewer, or will they bring a photographer along? And, if the photographer changes the time and says that they'll let the interviewer know, don't assume they will – always check. You don't want to get caught in the middle of a feud between a disorganised camera guy and an obsessively neat reporter.

Lastly, be aware that in the eyes of your interviewer your specialisation is probably a lot wider than *your* idea of your specialisation. You might have read widely and written on the American Civil War, but if America (and that's *anything at all* to do with America) happens to be in the news on the morning of your interview, be prepared to field any question, no matter how out of left field it might be.

How to be good at it

In a live interview, if you are not comfortable answering a question, just say so – or take the time to qualify your answer. There are no take-backs like there are in academic research interviews that have ethics approval. Although you can tell a journalist something is 'off the record' and not to be quoted directly or have your words attributed to you, we do question if there are any real 'off-the-record' moments in this world. Always be circumspect when there is a microphone in front of you or overhead: many a politician has regretted what they said to a 'hot mic' when they didn't think they were being recorded.

If the interview is not live, you can ask for a retake if you make a mistake. Don't make a habit of it and don't do it for every question, but if you make a mistake that you really don't want to go to air, just stop. Apologise and ask if you can do that question again. They won't mind – they want the interview to be accurate as much as you do.

One of the best things you can do to be successful in every interview format is to learn to speak in short grabs or sound bites. By all means convey the same information in all its glory and complexity, but be sure to take breaths and break your story into smaller sentences. If you are being recorded, it gives them somewhere to cut when they edit you, and, if you are talking to a print journalist, even they need a moment to take notes or to think of the next question. Long silences are to be avoided (although podcast hosts can edit them out), but short pauses are usually very welcome.

Make sure you listen to the question and answer it. Repeat it to make sure you're clear or ask for clarification if necessary. But don't do the politician's trick of pretending to listen to the question then giving the carefully rehearsed answer you intended to give all along. No one buys it, no one is convinced by it, and you are a researcher – you can do better than that.

With all formats, at the end of the interview, thank the interviewer for their time, make sure they have everything they need and emphasise that they can get in touch with you if they need anything more. Essentially, the more you do to make their life easier, the greater your chances are of surviving the cutting-room floor and even being contacted again in the future for another interview. Journalists quite like tip-offs and referrals too – they are always looking for that next breaking story – so, if you have a colleague who has something genuinely newsworthy to say, offer to put them in touch.

Very importantly, if your interview gets posted online, whether it be print, audio or video, be sure to link to it on your website, Tweet about it, post a link on your Facebook page and generally shout about it from the rooftops. Raising (and maintaining) awareness of you and your work is an ongoing thing. Keep the momentum up in any way you can.

And, in the very rare instance that, when the story comes out you find they've inadvertently gotten something wrong, remember that the media is not like academia – you have no right of reply, and trying to correct things in print at best muddies the waters and ends up confusing the message, and at worst just makes you look grumpy and bitter. So, while you can very politely contact the journalist to put them right, mostly you just have to grin and bear it and move on.

Notes on remote mode

In 2019, Professor Robert E. Kelly became a meme for having his kids break into his room chased by their frantic mother while being interviewed by a journalist. The juxtaposition between the academic in his suit and tie and his adorable, playful toddlers was considered hilarious at the time, but fast forward to the pandemic in 2020, and we are all potentially Professor Kelly now! Luckily interruptions by kids and cats have become normalised, so being interviewed from your home is not the high-stakes affair it used to be (despite the presence of

@ratemyskyperoom on Twitter, who will give you a score out of ten for your lighting and prop set-up). You can use a virtual background, but most look a little weird and will cut off the edges of your hair, especially if it is curly. Staging your background and your lighting is relatively simple. Here are a few tweaks (there's more at the end of the book in our section about speaking to camera).

- Position the camera at your eye level. Too high and you will look like you're at the bottom of a well; too low and you will loom. Take a few screenshots and adjust until you look OK.
- Don't have a window behind or in front of you. The light varies unpredictably, and most cameras cannot react fast enough, causing flickering. Unless you have a window to one side of your face with indirect light (called 'north light' in the northern hemisphere, 'south light' in the southern hemisphere), close the blinds and rely on artificial lighting.
- The screen in front of you will cast a bluish light. If you don't have enough light in the rest of the room, you will look like you're in a nightclub at 3 am (not the best look for anyone). Turn on the top light in the room and use a desk light to balance out the light from the screen. Turn down the brightness if you still see a bluish glow.
- You can get ring lights (round or square LED lights) that look like normal desk lamps now. Ring lights shed even light on your face and, if they have a soft pink setting that contrasts with the blue light from the screen, can even make you look fresh and youthful!
- Think about what is behind you. A bookshelf makes you look erudite, but make sure it's tidy. A shelf or credenza with a few ornaments or lamps is nice, but make sure that none of them are weirdly positioned behind your head. You don't want to look like you sprouted antlers or have a big lump emerging from your ear.

Further reading

The COVID-19 pandemic introduced us to the insides of many a pundit or academic's house as they began to be interviewed remotely from their homes instead of in the studio. During the pandemic, we amused ourselves following 'Room Rater' on Twitter (@ratemyskyperoom) – an account run by Claude Taylor and Jessie Bahrey. The account is beloved for its sometimes snarky commentary on people's house plant care, book shelves and lamp placement, and for spotting numerous 'cord violations'. People started to use Room Rater's eye for detail to improve their home set-up, and the team eventually produced a book called *How to Zoom Your Room*.[1] It's a tongue-in-cheek, fun guide to setting up almost every interior space in your house to be 'Zoom ready', and we recommend it highly! If you want to get the art of the interview down pat, again it can help to read books written for journalists. Inger likes *Interviewing: A Guide for Journalists and Writers*[2] by Gail Sedorkin, which manages to be both short and comprehensive and always practical.

Notes

1   Claude Taylor, Bahrey Jessie and Chris Morris, *How to zoom your room: Room rater's ultimate style guide*, Voracious, 2022.
2   Gail Sedorkin, *Interviewing: A guide for journalists and writers*, London: Routledge, 2011.

14 The socials: connecting online

TL;DR

- Social media platforms are the best way for researchers to connect with like-minded others and build professional networks.
- There is bound to be a channel that suits you – make it fun for yourself, not a chore.
- The ethical dimensions of social media use, including choice of platform, have real consequences for the discoverability of your work.

In a nutshell

This book is all about visibility. Our working theory is, if people know about your research, new connections and opportunities can emerge. If you embrace that idea, then there is no better tool for engagement than social media.

Social media platforms (the interfaces and server architecture that run them) come in all shapes and sizes now. There is bound to be at least one social media platform that suits the sort of topics you want to talk about, the amount of time you have available to devote to it and the sorts of audiences you want to

DOI: 10.4324/9781003197713-17

reach. In our opinion, the best kinds of platforms for researchers are those that enable you to post to a public profile, which aids discovery of your work.

We caution you to think very carefully about what platform(s) you use. Platforms controlled by corporate (or even political) interests should be approached with caution. At the time of writing, the most popular examples of corporately owned platforms include *LinkedIn*, *Facebook*, *TikTok* and *Twitter*, although that might have changed before this book is in print. Some sites exist purely to cater to different sides of the political spectrum; at the time of writing, the most popular examples are the right-wing-oriented platforms *Gab*, *Telegram* and *Parler*. Just before we finalised this book, some very large corporate sites are in a process of transition – specifically, Facebook (which is losing users) and Twitter (which was taken over by Elon Musk in 2022 with the intention of making it more 'free speech' friendly, provoking a mass exodus of people who feared this move would make the place unsafe and not fun). We are starting to see platforms that blend the corporate and political; at the time of writing, the best examples are *Truth Social* (which is really a mouthpiece for ex-president of the USA, Donald Trump) or *TikTok* (which has amorphous ties to the Chinese government).

In summary, and perhaps to simplify the situation massively, social media is in flux, with corporate, social and privacy interests in tension. In the creative soup, new, open forms of social media are gaining prominence. At the time of writing, 'federated' platforms like *Mastodon*, *Friendica*, *PeerTube*, *Pixelfed*, *Lemmy*, *Funkwhale* and *Bookwyrm* are starting to increase in popularity. Federated platforms are decentralised: anyone with the means and knowledge can spin up their own 'Instance' of a platform technology and let others use it. Federated social media platforms are underpinned by internet protocols that enable people to talk to each other and share content, no matter what server they are located on. The admins of the servers set the rules, and so set the culture and tone of discussion. For example, *Mastodon* is a micro-blogging platform similar to *Twitter* (although, crucially, not exactly the same). At the time of writing, several *Mastodon* servers exist for the purpose of hosting academics, such as *scholar.social* (designed to be a respectful and safe space) and *hcommons.social* (a place for humanities scholars). Some universities have started to explore providing *Mastodon* servers as a service to their community. By the time this book comes out, there might be hundreds more *Mastodon* communities for academics, organised by disciplines and interests. As a whole, these interconnected servers comprise a 'Fediverse' that is not owned by a single entity. By the time you read this, some of these servers and platforms may no longer exist and others will have emerged.

So – what is a researcher to do?

Our advice is to stop worrying about being on the 'right' platform and look for the one that suits you for now, keeping the following principles in mind:

1   **Any social media platform is also a form of control. Some forms of control are worse than others**. If a platform is owned by someone, be it a company or individual, they also control your access and, in some cases, own the content you put there – as well as its use and visibility. Functionally, there is no difference between a billionaire owning Twitter and a hobbyist making space for their friends on Mastodon: both can control your ability to put up a profile and kick you off if you behave in a way they don't like. BUT the way the technology is built matters. There is no way to migrate a Twitter profile away from Elon Musk's control as there is no other Twitter; you can move from one Mastodon server to another as many servers exist, independently in a 'Fediverse'.

2   **In this digital world, visibility is influence, but it is fragile. Any investment in building a network on**

a social media platform can be undone suddenly. Don't get too attached! We replaced this chapter, which was mostly about Twitter, at the last minute because we realised it was no longer current. The corporate takeover by Elon Musk changed the nature and tone of the platform abruptly. We believe it is on the way to becoming a place people don't want to be and may well die as a result. Social media is all about the people who are there. As we write, journalists, celebrities and academics are leaving *Twitter* in huge numbers. Without these people to provide content and interest, we predict *Twitter's* influence will wane. The publisher allowed Inger to rewrite this chapter in a hurry, five days after experiencing the mass exit of #AcademicTwitter… (for this revision, she relied on feedback from people who responded on *Mastodon* to her cry for help – thank you all!). We weren't able to go over the whole book and revise in the light of the new (at least to us) developments in federated social media platforms, so everything we said about social media previously should be read in relation to this chapter. Moving platforms can have big personal and professional costs for 'influencers' like Inger. Over 50,000 people were following her on *Twitter* before she abandoned the platform for *Mastodon* in November 2022. By the time you read this, she may have deleted her *Twitter* account. In the process of leaving *Twitter*, Inger abruptly became much less visible to the many academics who followed her there and probably less influential in academic circles as a result (for better or worse, Inger's 'social stats' were of interest to powerful people in academia and gave her opinions and ideas more weight). However, if *Mastodon* out-competes *Twitter* for academic eyes and attention, Inger will be able to rebuild this social media form of 'soft power'. On Mastodon she is not trapped the way she was on Twitter: she can take her followers to

another server if her current location (https://aus.social/@
thesiswhisperer) in the Fediverse becomes uncomfortable.
Luckily her blog had a huge email list so she can tell her
readers where she has 'gone', which leads us to our final
point.

3 **Focus on creating good, shareable 'content' in the
   form of essays, images and videos. Keep this content separate from the platform you use so people
   can always find you and your work.** Small businesses
   who relied on Facebook to provide a webpage and contact point were in trouble when people started leaving that
   platform. Likewise, some content creators invested a lot
   of time building followings by publishing long Twitter
   threads as an alternative to blogging and found their audience disappeared in a matter of days. An email list full of
   people interested in your work attached to a blog is much
   more useful than any social media presence. Marx was
   onto something when he talked about owning the means
   of production!

How to prepare

Start with The Google Test to see how visible you are on social
media already. Ask a friend to put your name into a search
engine to see what comes up. (Note: you need to ask someone
else to search you because Google will create what's called a
'filter bubble' for each person, showing results based on what it
knows about you. In other words, it's more likely to show 'you'
to you.)

There are always digital footprints, but some people's prints
are bigger than others. Explore the size and shape of your digital footprint by Googling yourself (make sure you do this

in 'private' mode so that you turn off the filters Google puts around your search – some browsers may allow this better than others). If you don't appear on the first page, you might need to search for more than just your name. Inger knows someone who shares a name with a very famous footballer who needs to add his university name to a search to see anything at all!

Assess the results of your self-Googling carefully. Does a casual search for your name make you look 'professional', or are many of the links about your private life? Do you see any social media handles in the results? Remember that Google is corporate too, so its algorithm privileges accounts on corporate platforms like *LinkedIn*. If you are not on one of those corporate platforms, you may not appear at all. Switch to image search and see how many versions of your happy, smiling face appear. Are these photos of you are ones you are happy to see online?

Now – and this is a really important step – describe your research in six words. Just six words. Then put these words into the search box and observe the results. Do any of your papers or articles appear? If you are not on the first or second page of the search results, even with a bit of tweaking, you are effectively invisible.

This is a very simple but extraordinarily useful exercise. The six-word Google test replicates what a television or radio producer, or a newspaper or online publication editor does when they are looking for an expert to write, speak, comment or analyse an issue of the day. These people sum up the issue in a mere handful of words, put it in the Search box, then contact whoever comes up first. It is really as simple as that. By coming up with six words that represent your work, your life and even your personality, you are also taking that first step on the all-important road to managing your online 'researcher identity' (we could call this a 'researcher brand', but that's a bit on the nose because most of us are not looking to the socials for our livelihood).

We know that some people reading this book will be all over social media, right up to and including the latest platform, so we are not going to get into the mechanics of any single service, other than to say preparation depends on what format your digital presence is to take and the culture of the digital space you enter. For example, *Mastodon* has a more consent-oriented culture than *Twitter* does and provides a content warning tool for this purpose, so people scrolling feeds do not have to be exposed to posts which may be personally upsetting (or boring). Be a good citizen wherever you land. Watch how others behave and act accordingly.

How to be good at it

We could probably write a whole book on cool things you can do with social media, but we don't have time for that now. We'll aim to give you some useful starting points instead.

Social media tends to fall into two categories: reactive and proactive. Put simply, people tend to make themselves heard online either when something needs saying or when they have something to say. Preparing yourself to be reactive is easy – you just simply stay abreast of the news and any developments in your field. Read the newspapers, set up some alerts – both scholarly and newsy – and when something happens in your field of expertise, you pounce with a well-written, pithy comment. You are probably already aware that social media can be a distraction too. Inger finds putting on a timer when she goes for a 'little scroll on the socials' is a good way to avoid time being eaten.

Proactive social media is a little harder to do, but not prohibitively so. You can either decide that today is the day to share a research story with the world, so you plan it, write it (or maybe make a film or podcast about it), edit it, publish it somewhere and then share it on your chosen platform(s). Alternatively, you can decide that you have a research story that is worth sharing but not time sensitive. We suggest you go through the same process but save it in a folder on your desktop just waiting for the right time to post it. That folder can also be filled with other stories, ideas for posts, even pictures – all waiting for the right time to see the light of day. This folder is also a bit of insurance against that inevitable eventuality – the fact that inspiration never strikes when you need it. So, when you realise that you haven't been online for a while and your followers are expecting something new from you, you simply open up your folder of good ideas, pick something out, change the date, tweak any time-specific references if necessary and post it.

Choosing a screen name is important – if you can secure one that is close to or the same as your name, great! If you don't want to go by your name, perhaps a nick name is a better option (Inger's students at RMIT called her 'The ThesisWhisperer', so she took the nickname she was given!). Whatever you do, try to use the same name across all the platforms you use so that you increase discoverability of your social feeds.

You can work in words, video and sound. Some of your webinars might be the perfect starting point for creating content, and most of the hosting and publishing options are free or low cost. If you're stuck for ideas, find some of your peers and colleagues who are already online and look at what they get up to. Creativity is at least partly theft, as they say. We do just want to spend a bit of time talking about blogging though, mostly because Inger's been doing it for over 12 years and it's our favourite type of content to make.

Blogs

If *Twitter* is the fast food of social media, then blogging is much more akin to the slow food movement – a good blog post will always be much more considered, planned and in depth than a quick, throwaway post. We encourage you to give at least a little thought about who your intended audience is, why they come to read your blog and what they are expecting from you.

You can really do a lot with a blog; your blog posts can link through to your original research for those who want to explore in greater depth. You can add comments to promote a conversation about an issue or gather feedback. Blogging frees you from formal 'academic' styles of writing. Try to express your preferred writing style in a couple of words before you start writing so you set the 'tone' (for example, Inger aims for 'Conversational, but smart. Occasionally rude.').

Blog posts have a lot in common with what are called opinion pieces – or sometimes 'analysis' – in newspapers and magazines, and their online equivalents. If you're comfortable with stirring up debate, even controversy, and expressing an opinion rather than just communicating facts, there is a seemingly insatiable audience out there for this format. We assume you will be producing expert opinion backed up by facts and will help inform the public debate. We strongly recommend you work within your academic circle of competence if you seek to inform debate in this way. If you 'swim in your lane', your university is more likely to back you up if you get sued, but don't count on it. Make sure you are at least passingly familiar with your local laws around defamation and slander.

Simon often issues a challenge to his students to write 'the perfect story' – this is a tick-the-box checklist of tips, tricks and techniques that journalists often use to being their stories alive. The opening of the story has to be great to catch the eye and keep the attention of your reader so we're after an amazing title, a killer opening line and a stunning first paragraph. And, of course, this goes full circle when you finish your piece with a killer closing line. And, while we're on the topic of circles, the circular structure is one of the most satisfying and rewarding structures you can use; start in one place, head off and cover every issue you can think of on the topic, but end up at the point you began at as you explain the outcome of the story. In between there's a whole load of little details that make for great writing: characters that come alive with quotes and anecdotes, colourful backgrounds that set the scene and startling statistics that really hammer home the impact of the story.

We encourage you to be brave within your circle of competence because expert opinion is something we desperately need – far too often what is presented to the world as informed opinion these days actually has no basis in fact and can, in some cases, be quite misleading. So take a deep breath, be prepared to ride out any potential backlash and write to let us all know what you think on your blog – or for that matter, your video or podcast. Making the world a better place is not necessarily an easy ride, but it's a step the rest of us will be eternally grateful to you for making.

Connecting

The content of your posts, videos, podcasts or whatever is only half the story. Whatever social media channel(s) you have decided to use, you should aim to build up a professional network so you can share and learn from like-minded others. When you first join a new platform, summarise your areas of interest (six words, remember?) and start searching for people – don't forget that many platforms use hashtags (#) to organise searches. Follow whomever you come across if their work is even vaguely related. Start talking to these people; hopefully they will follow you back and you can deepen your conversations. Over time you might make friendships that leap into the physical world. Be generous and help others whenever you can. Trust that just by sharing your nerdy self you will find others who share your interests and passions. You'd be surprised how collegiate other academics can be online. In our experience, those academics who aren't collegial, tend to find it hard to be there at all and will fade away in time.

To increase the possibility of connecting with like-minded others, share your digital presence in all your content. There is no reason why we shouldn't find all your 'socials', as they say, in your email signature file, at the bottom of your conference poster or across the last slide of your PowerPoint presentation – the one you leave strategically on the screen while everyone gathers up their belongings after your lecture.

Notes on remote mode

An online presence is not reliant on a physical presence or a specific location, so specific notes on remote mode are probably a bit redundant. We can only say that social media is one of the few options for getting your research out to a wider audience that is pandemic-proof. Enjoy it before they discover a variant that can infect the internet!

Further reading

For years Inger planned to write the definitive book on academics and social media, but Mark Carrigan pipped her to the post with his wonderful book *Social Media for Academics*[1] first published in 2016. We were even more impressed that Mark updated his book in 2019 and made it even more relevant than ever. We're deeply indebted to Mark for the content of this chapter. What we love about Mark's work is that he is 'platform agnostic' and doesn't get caught up in the trends of the day.

Instead, he delves deep into the 'why' of social media, outlining the many benefits and some of the perverse effects of the medium in the context of an academic career. Indispensable reading for anyone wanting to get really serious about building a research presence online.

Note

1   Mark Carrigan, *Social media for academics*, Thousand Oaks, CA: Sage Publications Ltd, 2019.

15 Lights, camera, research! Making short videos

TL;DR

- To be good at the format, you need to understand it first. Start by watching a lot of other people's videos and find out what you like.
- Break the process up into pre-production, production and editing phases. Pre-production starts with a good script.
- Get familiar with the different kinds of visual elements you can use to make a story – we provide a long list below.
- Don't forget to promote your video! Up to 50 per cent of videos put online are never viewed – it's a big waste of effort if you don't promote your work.

In a nutshell

There was a time when being asked to do a video would have represented a serious challenge to your average researcher – how on earth can I look and sound good on camera and get my message across in such a highly disposable format? Sure, we used to occasionally Skype someone on the other side of the world when the international project we were working on didn't have a budget for airfares, but this was the exception

DOI: 10.4324/9781003197713-18

not the rule. Then we had a pandemic. And now we are all movie stars in this work-from-home, Zoom-ridden, apocalyptic world that we have been forced to live in. So, let's make the most of that and use that experience to make sure we shine on YouTube, Vimeo, TikTok or whatever flavour-of-the-month video platform is coming next.

With all forms of communication, it is virtually impossible to master the format you are attempting if you don't understand it first. So, if you want to look good on YouTube and Vimeo or TikTok, the first thing you need to do is to watch an awful lot of YouTube and Vimeo or TikTok. Given the vast array of content out there, you might want to narrow down your viewing habits a little – we'd suggest avoiding the cute kitten videos and instead concentrate on content in areas that are related to yours. Try to find content that has a similar audience to the one you are hoping to attract. In fact, it's highly likely some of your peers or colleagues already have content out there, so that might make a very good place to start.

You will notice that academics use video communication for all kinds of purposes: to engage the public, to put teaching content up as an alternative way to access insights in a paper, to comment on the news of the day, to promote their books and so on. Done well, a popular video channel can really help your career as videos are more likely to be accessed than other forms of academic communication. Look for what works and what doesn't work on screen – both in terms of content and style of delivery.

Once you are abreast of the conventions in your particular area of research, think about how you can make it work for your purposes. The two things that should be front of mind here are *short* and *visual*. No one wants to watch a 2-hour video of someone just sitting and talking to their webcam. So have a bit of a brainstorm and work out what in your research lends itself to a visual presentation and what can be conveyed in a relatively short period of time.

Do you have existing visual material – photographs, maps, plans, charts, video footage, a well-designed PowerPoint display – that can be used on screen? And what are the exciting parts of your research that could be explained in 2 minutes, 5 minutes or even 10 minutes? If you really can't think of something that you could get across to an audience in a few minutes, maybe think about breaking it up into a series of short videos that make a series. Just remember that your viewers might not necessarily watch all of the series, nor even view the episodes in their intended order, so try to make each segment as stand-alone as possible.

How to prepare

Throwing something together in the hope that it will end up looking good is pretty much like aiming for failure from the start. Think of your short YouTube and Vimeo videos as mini-documentaries. Divide the process into pre-production, production and post-production, and have a plan. To make your video look good, you will almost certainly need access to technology and resources, so work out what you need and be prepared to buy or borrow whatever you need to achieve a great outcome. And take your time. The logistical complexity of a good video means that good results cannot be rushed. If you really have to, you can hastily throw together a quick speech or knock off a short article in a few hours, but it will always be better if you spend more time.

Pre-production means gathering up the materials you need to make your video. Everything starts with script – even if you are producing a 100-per cent visual presentation (images set to music, for example). If you are working alone, a script helps you get clear in your head what you are hoping to achieve; with collaborators, a script helps you communicate your vision.

Your script can then generate all sorts of things – a storyboard if you want to plan the look of the video, shot lists if you want to organise how you are going to film it, equipment lists and so on. There are all sorts of different ways you can format a script and you can spend a long time learning how to do it in Hollywood style. But here's what we think: so long as you and your collaborators can understand it, you can format a script in any way you like.

The script has a secondary function as a filter – it makes you think about, and express in words, anything you want to see on screen. No matter how complex, profound or earth-shattering your ideas are, if they can't be expressed in words on paper, they probably can't be filmed and represented visually on screen either. A script can save you so much time by showing you what is feasible and what is not.

Once you have your script, you move into the next phase of the production process where you film whatever needs filming and gather any other visual or audio resources you need. It is at this point that you learn that nothing ever happens as quickly as you think it will and, if technology can go wrong, it will. Patience, planning and a good contingency plan for everything are what you need here. So slowly and surely gather your material. And don't be afraid to have too much at this stage; that's what the editing process is for.

Representing research on screen can come in in all shapes and sizes, but generally there are some tried and tested techniques.

- **Presenting straight to camera**. This is usually you, as the expert, talking straight down the barrel of the lens.
- **Interviews**. Often in the field/on location, these are conversations with people in the know or affected by the issue at hand.
- **Background/establishing shots**. If you are making a video about climate change, just introduce your subject with

cracked soil or sun-bleached landscapes, and we'll know what you are talking about.

- **Cutaways**. These are short, often fairly close-up shots that are used to break up longer shots – think gesturing hands or close-ups of eyes slotted into an interview to alleviate any potential viewer boredom.
- **Objects**. Static or moving shots of objects can form part of your work.
- **Still images** (photographs, paintings, prints, etc.). Most editing software enables you to 'pan and scan' across images. Making a still image 'move' is a favourite technique of documentary film-makers and is an amazingly effective way to add life to your video – check out the section about making good-looking graphics at the end of the book for more ideas.
- **Archival footage**. If you're a historian and there is an existing film of the period you are talking about, this is a perfect way to illustrate your argument.
- **Animations**. These are a nice way of expressing difficult scientific processes or concepts. There are some good web tools that help you make simple animations, but they can even be done in PowerPoint.
- **Schematics/diagrams/charts**. Not the most exciting thing you could see on screen, so use these sparingly and check out our section on making good-looking visuals at the end of the book for more ideas.
- **Narration**. This is the mainstay of a lot of documentaries – either you on camera providing the narration or the classic, off-camera 'voice of God' narration (this is where everyone wishes they had the budget to be able to hire Morgan Freeman).
- **Music**. A musical soundtrack can be used to liven up visual filler shots. Remember copyright rules apply to music as well as images! Anything more than 10 seconds long will need permission.

- **Sound effects**. You might go to the country to an inter-view dairy farmer, but fail to get the perfect cow sound you wanted – there is no shame in inserting mooooo.mp3 from whatever online sound effects resource you can find.
- **Silence/'atmos track'**. A real professional touch here: if you are out filming in the field, record 60 seconds of 'silence' and then loop it under your edited interview to cover any gaps, joins or audio dropouts.

Once you've filmed your content and gathered all the other material you'll need, you do a 'paper edit' – a similar process to the planning and scripting stage. This means logging all the material you have gathered and working out how you are going to assemble everything on paper. A good tip is to use a log table (see Table 15.1), with a column for the time, description of the content and the file name.

A paper edit and log table will save you time and even money, and will make the whole process so much more efficient.

How to be good at it

Most short videos tend to be quite traditional in a 'beginning, middle and end' kind of way. Generally, research hinges on

Table 15.1 Log table sample

Time	Description	Filename(s)
00:00:00–00:00:13	Long shot of cow in field with voice-over	CowInField.mpg Mooooo.mp3 Voiceover1.mp3
00:00:13–00:00:25	Me talking to camera about the cow cult	Cowcult1.mpg AngryMoo.mp3

facts and figures so these will be more important than capturing a mood or challenging narrative stereotypes. You should feel free to experiment, of course, but be aware of the world you are operating in and the demands of the audiences you hope to attract. Unless you are a film-making researcher, you are not an expert. Set your expectations accordingly.

Always aim for a professional finish – this means high-quality images and, even more importantly, crisp, clean sound. It's interesting that the MTV revolution made us all a bit more visually forgiving with things like jump cuts and rough camera work, but throw in a badly recorded soundtrack and you'll have your audience turning off in droves. The good news is that most of the technology you need to look and sound good will work on your average laptop and some of it is even free. We would include a list, but by the time you read this book the software and technology landscape will have changed. We do know the trend is to increasing ease of use so we feel confident you can research your way out of this problem.

Give some consideration to how your audience is going to look at your video. It's more likely your video will be viewed on a mobile phone, maybe a tablet, than on a laptop or desktop. This means your beautifully shot footage may well be reduced down to something that's not much bigger than a thumbnail, so go for head and shoulders 'talking heads' or carefully constructed graphics over sweeping vistas of wide, brown plains.

You can learn a lot from film and television that is relevant to your YouTube and Vimeo videos. Shot sizes telegraph the intention of the director in a movie, and you can do the same thing in your work. The longer or wider the shot, generally the more action we will see and the more objective the audience is invited to be. The closer we are to the performers, the more emotion we should expect to see on the screen, inviting the audience to have a more subjective experience. An 'explainer' video, for example, will use what's called a 'mid shot' – that's your head and shoulders on screen and little more. Check out our section about speaking on camera, at the back of the book, if you are setting up camera shots like this.

Notes on remote mode

- You can use your video in a couple of ways. You can embed it, or embed a link to it, in a website so that it just shows as part of that website, or you can have your own channel on a video platform that people go to for content.
- If you decide to have your own channel, unless your first foray into filming has totally put you off, think about your next video as soon as you have finished your first. Ideally you want to set up a channel that has a few videos on it and that is replenished and added to fairly frequently. Not only do you want an audience that comes back regularly to see what you've come up with next, but there's something just a bit odd about a YouTube channel with only one video on it.
- Once you have produced your video, you need to attract an audience in what is a very, very crowded marketplace. Producing even the most basic of short clips requires time, effort, technology and sometimes money; so if you are going to go to the trouble of marshalling these resources, surely it's worth making sure a few people at least glance at it. You need to stand out from the crowd – for all the right reasons. In fact, getting an audience is almost as important as generating content. Simon once met a researcher looking at the impact of content on YouTube, and he had unearthed the startling fact that, at that time, 50 per cent of videos on YouTube were never watched. This is worth repeating – they were *never* watched. That means that not even the person uploading the video, nor their friends and relatives, had bothered to play the video. Unbelievable!

- Ideally, your digital screen content will be part of a larger social media and marketing strategy so you can use your Twitter presence or your blog or website to alert your existing audiences to exciting new content they can look at. If it isn't, or if you're just starting out, use whatever you can to spread the word.
- Put a link in your signature file to your YouTube or Vimeo content. Mention your digital presence in your lectures and put links in the notes you distribute at the end. Essentially, overcome any hesitation towards blatant self-promotion or shyness and do whatever it takes. Self-promotion has become more normalised in academia as the whole profession has become more competitive.

Further reading (and buying)

There's a reason why 'videographer' is a profession that actually employs a lot of aspiring film-makers: making excellent video content is really hard work and highly technical. We recommend you start with *Film Directing: Shot by Shot*[1] which has examples of story boards from many famous movies and breakdowns of how to achieve the same look. May we gently suggest that if you are going to get super serious about film-making, you will need to invest in a very expensive camera as your phone just isn't going to cut it. If you do invest, make sure you buy extra batteries and storage cards as they are always the first things to fail on a location shoot!

Note

1   Steve D. Katz, *Film directing: Shot by shot – 25th anniversary edition: Visualizing from concept to screen*, Studio City, CA: Michael Wiese Productions, 2019.

16 Listen up! Podcasting your research

TL;DR

- Podcasting is one of the most effective ways to build a following – in our experience, podcast listeners are the most loyal (and affectionate!) of any online audience.
- Start with why: who is listening to your podcast and what do they want to get out of the experience? Maybe even more important: where are they listening? The format of your show should meet the audience where they are.
- You don't need a lot of fancy equipment to get started, but it surely makes the process easier if you are willing to invest in a good microphone and some software.
- All good podcasts rest on good show notes: script your way to podcast success!

In a nutshell

Podcasting is simply radio translated to the digital era. A podcast is a digital sound file delivered through a webpage or a podcast player app on your phone. The most popular podcast app at the time of writing is Apple podcasts, but streaming services like Spotify have seen the potential of the market in podcast

DOI: 10.4324/9781003197713-19

listeners and have started to commission artists to exclusively deliver via their platform. Podcasting is one of the most rapidly growing social mediums; savvy brand 'entrepreneurs' have been jumping onto for a while now. Everyone from Barak Obama to Paris Hilton have a podcast these days, why not you?

The reason why podcasting has grown so rapidly is quite simple: advertising. Like radio before it, podcast advertising is extremely effective because of the nature of the audience engagement. Podcasting is an intimate medium – your voice is literally in someone's ears. And you might be in their ears anywhere: while they are driving, exercising, doing housework or gardening because you can multitask while listening to a podcast in ways that you can't while watching a video or reading a blog post. The intimacy of podcasting as an experience sets up what researchers have called a 'parasocial' relationship, where listeners feel like they know the host(s) personally (https://doi-org.virtual.anu.edu.au/10.1080/19376529.2020.1870467). As a result (and Inger can attest to this personally), podcast listeners are one of the most loyal and engaged audiences you will find. While other social media, such as Twitter, can attract a range of critics, podcasting tends to make fans. We highly recommend podcasting if you want to do serious research communication over an extended period of time and set yourself up as a known expert in a specific knowledge space.

How to prepare

Anyone who can record a sound file and upload it to the internet can be a podcaster. Listeners can subscribe or follow a podcast and see the latest episodes appear in a playlist. Unlike other social mediums, podcasting is not yet dominated by algorithmic feeds and search structures. If you put a post on Facebook or Twitter, for example, algorithms decide how many people see the post and when. By contrast, a subscriber sees podcast episodes as they are released, which makes it a more reliable social media method for distributing your research.

The key to making a good podcast is good sound recording principles. Start with purchasing a decent microphone. While you can certainly record a podcast with your gaming headphone set, an external, stand-alone microphone is infinitely better. Don't record with wireless ear pods or similar: Bluetooth does not transmit all frequencies so you will sound like your head is in a bucket. If you have a guest, ask them to use a headset that actually plugs into their computer. Move the mic up to your mouth and sit relatively close. A good way to judge distance is to hold your hand perpendicular to the mic with your little finger resting on it; put your mouth near your thumb and it will be about right. Make sure you use headphones when you record so you can minimize any sound coming from the background, such as another person talking. While a lot of the software platforms will have echo control, they will struggle to remove all the effects of background noise.

You can get relatively good sound by making sure you record surrounded by soft surfaces, like carpet and curtains. You can soften sound by putting a towel over the surface of your desk and a baffle in front of your mic so the sound doesn't bounce off the screen; Inger uses egg cartons. In Figure 16.1, you can see Inger's towel and egg carton set-up for her monthly 'On The Reg' podcast: as you can see, your set-up can be quite 'home brew' and sound professional – no one will know! And very importantly, make sure you monitor your audio in your headphones not with your ears. Your ears are forgiving, and your brain can paper over the cracks without you even realising it. But your headphones hear *everything*!

When you have your sound file recorded, you may want to do some post-production work, like editing and manipulating sound levels. Most computers come with built-in software for

Figure 16.1 Inger's 'home-brew' podcasting set-up.

this purpose, or you can download any number of free sound editors. These editors are good for cutting in music or other clips and taking out/adding in sound. If you want to do fancier editing, such as removing all the filler words ('um, 'uh' and so on), consider investing in a transcription software service like

Descript or Otter.ai. These services enable you to turn a sound file into text and edit it like a word document, speeding up the editing process and giving you more control.

Finally, upload your file to the internet. You can go through the process of setting up a podcast RSS feed, or you can throw money at the problem by using a service like Buzzcast, which not only houses the file and any show notes but has built-in mastering to smooth out your sound levels and tools to add advertising material, if that's you want to do.

How to be good at it

Of course, good podcasting starts with good sound, but if you don't have good content, you won't go far. Every podcast should start with some kind of script so that you know what kind of journey you are taking your listener on when they plug you in their ears. Broadly speaking, there are two types of podcast script: chat and narrative. A chat-style podcast is just what it sounds like: one or more people get together and discuss a topic or conduct an interview. A narrative podcast is a story, maybe one that incorporates an element of mystery. You can do combinations of these two types by telling a documentary style of story with snippets of interviews and voice-overs.

In our experience, the narrative-style podcast is much harder to pull off, but perhaps suits research communication better than pure chat. It's hard to do a chat podcast on your own, but grab a buddy or two, and you have the raw ingredients for a good podcast because people love 'over-hearing' a conversation between people with a lot to say. A narrative podcast needs to be thought through carefully. In his book *Making Noise*, veteran radio producer Eric Nuzum reminds us that good stories consist of *images* in the listeners' minds – places where things happen and actions done by characters. Your characters can be people, or they can be inanimate objects... they are more interesting if they have flaws as well as strengths. Remember characters have to *want* something: even non-human things can be seen to want something, for instance, the COVID virus just wants to survive, but unfortunately it wants to survive in us. The flow in the COVID virus is the spike protein. A good science story about the COVID virus could start in just this way. The best way to resolve a story is to show us *change*: change in the self or change in the world.

We mentioned the para-social relationships that become possible with podcasting at the start of this chapter. Para-social relationships make for loyal listeners who will spread the word about your podcast. You can lean into this potential by developing a distinct broadcasting style of your own, disclosing a bit of private information (which makes you into a more well-rounded person), letting listeners into the podcast experience and responding to them, for instance by encouraging them to write in or send in sound files you play 'on air' (Inger uses www.speakpipe.com for this purpose).

Practically speaking, your script should be structured so that you capture the right information for creating some show notes (the blurb that appears with your podcast in a podcasting app). Below is the script structure Inger uses for her 'On The Reg' show with her friend Dr Jason Downs:

ON THE REG - Season 3

Episode Number:

Riverside Studio Link

Recording Date: dd/mm/2022
Recording Time: hh:mm - hh:mm
Release Date: dd/mm/2022
Reference:
Episode Summary for Buzzsprout Directory:

Intro: (3 minutes)
Inger is driving the bus 🚌 🚌

Welcome to On The Reg...

I'm Professor Inger Mewburn, from the Australian National University, but I'm better known as @Thesiswhisperer on the internet. And I'm here with my good friend Dr Jason Downs from La Trobe University for another episode of On The Reg, where we talk about work, but you know – not in a boring way. Practical, implementable productivity hacks to help you live a more balanced life. Before we get started, as always, we'd like to thank our podcast recording platform Riverside for supporting On The Reg by providing us with a free subscription in return for spreading the word about how good they are.

Welcome Jason... How have you been since we last caught up?
Jason:
Hi Inger... Good to see you again! Things have been......

......

......

......

...... So, what about you? How have you been?
Inger:

......

......

......

Work problems!
A problem you had to solve since last we spoke (30 minutes)

In this part of the show, we focus on one aspect of work and talk about the problems we've encountered. We like to analyse the problems, so sometimes we talk about the literature.

We also try to be practical, sharing our tips and hacks for solving the problems. We take it in turns to decide the actual problem, and this week it's Jason's turn.

Jason: *<Snappy title of problem>*
Description of the work problem:
Why it is a problem in universities and why it might be a problem for others:
How you dealt with it...:

What we've been reading
Inger:
Description of thing – book/article/website:
What you found interesting/unusual/frustrating about it:
How it can help others:

Jason
Description of thing – book/article/website:
What you found interesting/unusual/frustrating about it:
How it can help others:

The two-minute tip

Inger
This is in honour of one of the techniques that David Allen advocates in his Getting Things Done books. He argues that if you think up a task and it takes less than two minutes to complete, that you should do it then and there because it'll take longer to capture it in your task system, schedule time to do it and mark it as complete than it would if you just did it then and there.

My two-minute tip for this episode is....

Jason
My two-minute tip is......

Outro: 2 mins

Thanks for listening!

For those of you who might want to start your own podcast and are wondering which podcast recording platform to use, we use and recommend Riverside. The good folks at Riverside have provided us with a link that will offer new users a 20% discount. If you do decide to use Riverside, tell them that Inger and Jason sent you...

BTW – we love reviews. We'd love it if you could leave a review on Apple podcasts – we read every one and we use them to actively shape our show.

If you want to join us with a question, a great way to do that is to record it via our speakpipe page. You can find it at https://www.speakpipe.com/thesiswhisperer. We'd love to hear from you!

You can find us both on Twitter: @thesiswhisperer and @jasondowns

Notes on remote mode

Podcasts are a remote medium by default of course, but it's worth pointing out that podcasting is actually easier if the hosts are not co-located. You can use a range of teleconferencing software to record hosts in different locations starting with Zoom if that's the only tool you have available to you. We don't recommend Zoom as connectivity issues can really affect the sound you produce. Instead, use a platform where you can record each person onto their own computer, but create a synched up file in the cloud. At the time of writing, Inger is using Riverside, but you can get the same service via other platforms like Squadcast and Zencaster.

Further reading (and buying)

Podcasting is a new medium, but there are already some good books on the market. We have already mentioned Eric Nuzum's *Make Noise*[1], and you cannot get a better book on how to make compelling sound stories in our opinion. Another excellent reference is *The Power of Podcasting: Telling Stories Through Sound* by Siobhan McHugh. McHugh does a more scholarly analysis of the potentials of podcasting and offers a range of useful case studies as inspiration.

Note

1 Eric Nuzum, *Make noise, a creator's guide to podcasting and great audio storytelling*, New York: Workman Publishing, 2020.

Part IV

Good to know

You've done all the hard work; you've put together presentations that will wow your audiences, but there are still a few things to worry about – 'the fine print' if you like. In this section, we tackle some of the technical complexities of producing sound and images that apply to any presentation you might make. We also consider the broader context for all research communication. No research presentation exists in a vacuum – universities, and societies for that matter, are complex. You must constantly deal with other people's reactions to your work and pay due respect to rules and laws.

In this section, we'll take you through some basic principles of visual images and help you make great videos and audio presentations. We'll give you some advice on tackling questions and dealing with trolls – both in person and on the internet. Finally, we provide some advice for navigating the mysteries of copyright and IP (while this section was checked by experts in the field, be sure to check our advice against your university's guidelines and local country laws as we are not lawyers). This section is probably the start of what you need to know to become an expert research communicator, but hopefully, it will be a good foundation for your future fabulousness!

DOI: 10.4324/9781003197713-20

Appendix 1: Speaking to camera

Being able to confidently talk about your work in front of a camera is an essential skill. There was a time when it was just a matter of choice – maybe you needed to collaborate with someone in a different time zone, but the budget didn't run to an airfare, for example – but then the world changed and almost overnight it became an obligatory skill for any aspiring researcher. We don't know what the future will hold, but at the moment it looks like webcams are very much here to stay.

Of course, there is a very positive side to this new digital world; you can talk to anyone, anywhere, anytime. You can even replicate the old 'my door is always open' policy in platforms like Zoom, where you have your own room as a persistent link and people can pop in when they need a quick chat. As we've talked about throughout the book, this same technology can be used to replicate a one-on-one chat over coffee, a departmental staff meeting, a workshop or seminar, or even a keynote presentation to hundreds if not thousands of people.

Presenting live online

At the moment there are quite a few platforms for digital video chat, with a new one seeming to pop up every few weeks. Other

DOI: 10.4324/9781003197713-21

than the buttons and menus being in different places, most are remarkably similar and they all do pretty much the same thing, with the possible exception of online paid conference platforms which seem to specialise in making it tricky for presenters to enter. The good news is the technology you need to use them from your office or home and the peripheral devices that make you look good on screen are identical in every case.

A good online presenter makes the audience forget that they are staring at a screen, instead of listening to a person in the same room as them. At least, that's the dream. Certainly, you should make your audience feel relaxed and comfortable in your presence so that they are experiencing something as close to a conversation as you can get in the digital world. Because screen-based activities are more demanding for both speaker and audience, a successful online presenter will be able to compress what would normally have taken them hours to say into a few short minutes. Or, if you are going to present over a matter of hours, you will need plenty of breaks and activities to break up the time.

If you are sharing documents or doing anything fancier – such as combining PowerPoint with a live camera – you need to make sure it happens seamlessly and effortlessly. Ideally, a successful online presenter shouldn't have to ask, 'Can everyone hear me?' – but equally, because technology isn't perfect, they shouldn't be fazed when it turns out that not everyone can hear them.

As with all public speaking, being calm and in control is what you should aim for. In person this would normally mean being thoroughly prepared, having rehearsed your speech, put your slide deck together, anticipated tricky questions and so on, but online there is also that nagging thought: what if the technology fails me? Every platform has some sort of test or preview function, so test everything beforehand. If you are scheduled to be online at 12 pm, you should be all ready to go with audio and video checked at 11:50 am with your finger hovering over the Join Meeting button. Always allow yourself enough time between your test and when you are due to meet for a quick reboot if necessary.

And make sure you are 100 per cent ready. How is your background looking – is the 'stage' all set? Are any files you need to share open and ready to go? If you need physical props, are they nearby? Bottle of water on hand just in case (but no glasses of water next to the keyboard – especially when you are nervous). A clock of some sort close to your eyeline is not a bad thing if you are delivering a timed presentation. Looking down at the clock at the bottom of your computer screen can be tricky to do mid-presentation and means you have to take your eyes off the audience. Analogue clocks are better than digital as they more clearly show how much time you have left at a glance.

Looking good on camera

There are two equally important elements that contribute to success in delivering a good online presentation. The first is the technology; the second is you.

You don't need to spend an absolute fortune – sometimes cheap and cheerful equipment will outperform expensive toys if used well – but you do need to know what you are doing. You will need a camera, some audio equipment and (this is where you can really make a difference) some lighting.

The image of you the viewer sees needs to be as close to the view they would normally get when talking to you in person, which generally means eye level – not too high, not too low. It's a good idea if your camera is as close as possible to your monitor so that when you look at your colleagues on screen, they see an image of you looking them in the eye, or at least that's how it looks to them. A laptop with a built-in webcam at the top of the screen will do OK, although, as most of us tend to have our laptops on our desks and look down at them, you'll need to elevate your laptop a bit to bring it up to eye level. There are cheap stands at most office supply places that prop up your laptop so the screen is at eye height – you'll need an external keyboard and mouse to work on your machine, but your neck will thank you! If you're using individual components like external monitors and a camera on a tripod, you'll need to move them around until you can easily see everything as you present.

You can use the built-in microphone and speakers on your computer for audio, but that means your colleague can hear everything around you and your conversation can be heard all over your office. Not only is that tricky for privacy and concentration, but it's hell if you're in a shared office or, worse still, working from home with a dog that loves to bark and two kids under school age who like to sing the *Play School* theme at the top of their voices. A headset – either wired or wireless – will pipe the conversation right into your ears and pick up your voice without also picking up too much of the background noise.

Lighting is what really separates the old hands from the newbies. Again, it doesn't need to be expensive or complicated, what's more important is how you use it. You can go all out and light yourself cinematically (key light from one direction for strong shadows, fill light to even things out and a backlight to separate you from your background), and there are plenty of websites to help you do this. Really, as long as you have a lot of soft light (diffuse light that doesn't throw harsh shadows), you'll look good. Some cameras have a light built in, but even the little ring lights that some of them have are still too directional. Go for external lights.

It's much better to get the biggest, brightest lights you can find. There are some amazingly affordable LED lights available online these days – they have become the new fashion in pandemic homewares! Stand them about halfway between you and whichever wall you are facing and point them at the ceiling. The light bounces off the ceiling and gives you a nice, soft, even light that brings out the features of your face without casting harsh shadows across it and lights the background evenly at the same time. Just be aware that different types of lighting (incandescent globes, LED lights, fluorescent tubes, for example) give out different sorts of light (the technical term is colour temperature), and when you mix colour temperatures, it can give weird results. So, if you are going to use a couple of LED lights, make sure you switch off all the other lights in the room.

The second side half of the equation is, of course, you. Or at least your head and shoulders, as that's pretty much all that we will see of you. And, before you ask, yes: pyjama bottoms with a shirt and tie is definitely an acceptable look for the home broadcaster. TV newsreaders have been getting away with it for years!

Let's start with how you look. And that includes your background. Are you wearing smart but casual clothes in neutral colours? Are the colours of your clothing sufficiently different from your background so you don't do a bit of a 'cloak of invisibility' number? Have you remembered to avoid thin stripes that will 'strobe' on screen or dangly jewellery that will get caught in your headset or rub against your microphone?

What can be seen on the screen behind you can also contribute to the image you are presenting. Is your background (think of it as your set or location in theatrical or cinematic terms) nice, clean and uncluttered so that your presentation looks professional? Is there anything there that shouldn't be visible – clients' confidential details, for example? Digitally inserted backgrounds are OK. But *only* OK. They always look fake and some of the worst examples create very ugly halos around your head as you move. If your office really is so unsightly that it needs to be hidden from public view, maybe consider investing in a cheap, portable green screen to hang behind your head so that, if you really have to use a digital background, at least it will look good.

Performing on camera

Now for the tricky part – how you 'perform'. In cinematic terms, you will be seen in something between a mid-shot and a close-up. This is quite an intimate shot, and it means that the effect is more like chatting over a coffee in a café than it is standing and lecturing in a theatre filled with hundreds of students. A bad hair day, and any pimples and blemishes will be highly visible (if that kind of thing bothers you), and people will see you fiddle with your nose or mouth, so resist the urge. Expressions will be magnified, especially if you are being shown as a 'big head' on a screen when everyone else is in the room. Watch out for eye-rolls and sighs!

Always know what you will be seeing and hearing. Will you be presenting to a screen full of happy, smiling faces, Brady Bunch style, or will you have the worst of all worlds – a tiny box at the bottom of the screen that says nothing more than 'Number of participants: 27'? You will have to work in both situations at different times, but forewarned is forearmed, as they say.

Do you have any housekeeping instructions to give out? Do you have to tell your audience to mute their mics? If you have a complicated running order or need reminders of key elements, maybe try printing them out in a nice, large font and Blu-tack the sheet next to your camera/monitor set-up. Inger uses colour-coded run sheets in Google Docs, with click-throughs to her individual slide decks. We've included an example in Table A.1, using different grey shades for each colour-coded row, from one day of a writing retreat.

Table A.1 Sample run sheet for an online workshop

Writing retreat Day 1: Finding the storyline Muddiest Point document	
9:00–9:20	Instructions and settling in SMART Goals tracker
9:40–10:00	Meet your writing room partners!
10:00–10:30	Write an abstract and clarify the through line for your paper Resource: Tiny text explainer
10:40–12:00	Fill in Deep work SMART Goals tracker Deep work: session 1
12:00–1:00	Lunch! (The Zoom meeting will stay active)
1:00–2:00	How to write (much) faster Resources: • Blog post with paper structures • Snowflake move step process • Manchester Phrase Bank • Blog post on argument diagramming • Wikipedia page on argument mapping
1:30–3:45	Fill in Deep work SMART Goals tracker Deep work: session 2
3:45–4:00	Debrief

When it comes to question time, the usual rules of engagement apply online, but you have the added degree of difficulty of managing them technically. The chat box that all platforms have can be your friend here. Selecting who is to ask the next question, followed by the unmuting of their mic, and then the question itself can be quite clumsy, so why not just get people to type their questions into the chat box and you read them out? Of course, this also gives you a couple of added advantages: not only do you get to see the questions and read them out – a great way to play for time while you think of an answer – but there's no rule that says you have to answer them in the order they come in. Who could blame you for answering the easy questions first while you think through the answers to the hard ones?

Online presentations are no different to physical presentations where the legalities are concerned – don't use anything (words, ideas, images) unless it is yours or you have asked for and been granted permission from the copyright holder to use it. If this is the case, make sure you acknowledge (see our section on IP at the end of the book for more detailed rules). And be very careful; with online presentations there is the very real possibility that you may be recorded, so the old excuse of 'I'm *sure* I didn't say that' just won't wash.

Finally, this format is fast becoming the most essential kind of teaching skill in an academic toolkit, so embrace the chance to practise when you are offered the chance to do one.

Appendix 2: Answering questions and dealing with trolls

It's always a good sign if listeners ask you questions at the end of a presentation. If they were engaged enough to formulate a question, you have done your job well and should pat yourself on the back. But question time can fill even the most seasoned presenter with dread. Questions are the ultimate test of how well you can think on your feet. Let's take some time to dwell on the kinds of questions – and questioners – you can expect to encounter.

Questions

First off: it's common for questioning in academia to be adversarial, even aggressive. Many academics regard questioning as a martial art; some academics have a black belt in it after sparring for decades with colleagues. Some love to show off their hard-won battle skills, especially on unsuspecting students.

In our experience, the questioning you get outside of academia can be equally difficult. While you might meet less seasoned academic warriors, you can meet people who are hostile to your point of view, which requires you to get out of the expert mindset and deploy empathy.

While we hope that most questions you encounter are motivated by curiosity, there are some forms of questions designed to throw you off your game. Problematic questions tend to fall into different types. There is power in being able to recognise a problematic question type. As Inger's therapist is fond of saying, 'name it to tame it'. Once you mentally categorise a question, you are in a stronger position to answer in a powerful way. In the book *How to Give Winning Presentations* by Jim Macnamara and Brenda Venton (which Inger saved from the recycling bin when it was being weeded from the Australian National University (ANU) collection), there is a list of nine types of questions and some strategies for answering them.[1]

Here they are (updated to remove sexist language!).

- **The concealed objection**: a question asked in bad faith that is actually a refutation of your position. It's not a question but an invitation to fight. This type of question puts you on your mettle to marshal more persuasive arguments, but recognise that sometimes you can't win as your questioner is likely to be holding deeply held beliefs that are difficult to shift.
- **The test question**: designed to probe your background knowledge or expertise, sometimes to discredit you. Women may find they get these questions more than men. You know your research better than anyone else – be confident in your expertise and answer as best you can. If the questioning persists, we think it's OK to shut it down, perhaps by offering to take up the discussion via email. Don't invite these kinds of questioners to talk to you later – there's often nothing to be gained if their intention is to belittle you.
- **The display question**: not really a question but a display of knowledge, sometimes intended to intimidate. The best way to handle the question, we've found, is to ask the questioner if that was a comment or a question. If they say it's a question, ask them to rephrase it in a shorter form.
- **The challenge question**: more a territorial dispute than a question. This questions your right to do the research in the first place – usually on grounds of methodology. This type of question is similar to the test question above, but more

confrontational. While test questions probe your bone fides to carry out the research properly, the challenge question is about the research itself. Answer as best you can, but you may have to agree to disagree with the questioner if you can't persuade them. It can be confronting to tell people 'thanks but no thanks' for offering their views, but practise doing this a couple of times and it will get easier, we promise!

- **The defensive question**: a question by someone who might be affected by what you are suggesting. Research that shifts paradigms can be challenging to some people who are stuck in particular kinds of methods and assumptions. If you are doing this kind of research, you will quickly get to know where these sticking points are. The only advice we have is that you need to be sure of your reasons and able to explain them clearly. Again, be prepared to give up the fight if it looks hopeless – as someone once said, 'It's very hard to persuade a person to think differently if their pay cheque depends on it.'
- **The off-the-record question**: often asked by journalists who want background to a piece. Be careful how you answer – as we said in Chapter 13 on media interviews, nothing is ever totally off the record!
- **Yes or no questions**: designed to force you to oversimplify. You can only persist in refusing to oversimplify and explain your reasons and evidence again. If you are repeatedly challenged in this way, it's now a dominance move. Don't get sucked into a pointless fight – move on to the next question.
- **'No-win' questions**: no matter how you answer, you are in trouble. Move on!

Online trolling

If you work in an area like climate science or gender studies, it's highly likely you will attract trolls to your public presentations or when you speak online. However, in these fractious times, all of us are potential targets for trolling. Just being an academic with an opinion (or worse, a female or trans person *and* an academic) can make you a target. We could write a whole book on this problem alone, but we only have space for a short section to help you recognise trolling in action.

In the 21st century, trolling has evolved. When online trolling emerged at the turn of the century, it was primarily disaffected individuals. Individual trolling still exists, and, sadly, it can even come from other academics, but for some years now, trolling has been a highly co-ordinated practice. So-called 'brigading', or 'piling on' to one individual who has dared to voice an opinion, is a tactic used by groups of trolls. These troll groups can be organised around racist or sexist ideologies and, in a more sinister turn, by actors who are either directly controlled by state actors or allowed and encouraged by state actors for geopolitical or business ends. Co-ordinated trolling is designed to disrupt and agitate by focusing anger on an individual. Harassment can bleed out of online spaces and be genuinely terrifying, especially if it includes threats to your family, your job or even your life.

There's a difference between a genuine question and a person intent on trolling. Trolls are not interested in your answers; they want attention. Trolls tend to display a high level of what psychologists call 'The Dark Tetrad': Machiavellianism, narcissism, psychopathy, direct sadism and vicarious sadism (with the sadism components most common).[2] Remember a sadist *enjoys* inflicting pain on others. The best way to stop a troll is to not give them what they want: your distress.

While some people like to engage with trolls and believe they can educate them, we are sceptical of this approach for the working researcher. Trolls want to take up your time and energy – emotional and otherwise. This energy is best invested in doing your research. We believe the most potent form of communication is silence – from you. But we do believe, in line with advice from writers on trolling such as Ginger Gorman,[3] that being an active bystander is important. While you might not respond to people trolling you, it can help to send messages of support when others are under attack. Likewise, anyone you see engaging in trolling, whether it is aimed at you or someone else, can be blocked, muted and/or reported. Reporting trolls en masse to shut them down is a remarkably effective technique. Of course, you can have genuine conversations with non-academics online, and sharing our knowledge is one reason to be on social media in the first place.

Trolling tactics

Here's a list of generic trolling types so you can learn to spot and label trolling tactics. If you recognise what they are trying to do, you're less likely to waste your time.

The reply guy

The reply guy wants to tell you why you are wrong or correct you – all the time. The reply guy replies to almost every post you make, especially if you are a woman. The reply guy maybe thinks his attention is … flattering? We are not sure. Every woman with a large enough profile will have a couple of reply guys dogging their every move – Inger has blocked at least 100 on Twitter.

The Twitter account @9ReplyGuys identified nine specific types of comments common to most reply guys in 2018.[4] Look out for them.

'They mean well' types:
- The Life Coach: offers unsolicited advice on, well, everything.
- The Cookie Monster: he loves women, he has daughters, #notallmen.
- The Mansplainer: usually starts with 'Well, actually ...' and then proceeds to tell you about your own research.

The ones who think they are 'focusing on the real problems':
- Tone Police: he's just asking you to mind your language, ladies!
- Himpathy: any criticism of men is a witch hunt.
- The Prestige: defends men who are high status.

The ones clearly operating in bad faith:
- The Gaslighter: 'It's not that bad. And if it is, you deserve it.'
- The Sea-lion: asks endless questions in bad faith (see below for more).
- Trolls, Creeps and Fools: straight up sexism because 'covert misogyny just wasn't enough'.

What-aboutery

This is the double backflip of troll argumentative tactics! Basically, this troll is trying to make you look like a hypocrite without actually refuting your argument. The so-called 'debates' about #notallmen or #alllivesmatter are examples of What-aboutery, but it's best understood through a theoretical example. Say you are giving a talk about your research on violence towards women. A troll using What-aboutery might ask you about what you found out about violence towards men. If you try to tell the troll that you didn't look at violence towards men, the troll will use your refusal to answer as 'evidence' that you aren't really interested in researching violence and can't have anything useful to say on the topic because you didn't study other forms of violence too.

Concern trolling

This occurs when a troll is actually trying to argue with you while appearing to agree with you. They often offer covert criticism in the form of faux concern. For example, they include a person who criticises others about their weight by appearing to care about their health and a person who expresses concern about young people making decisions about gender identity too early by expressing worry that they will regret it later. The more pernicious form of concern trolling is Just Asking Questions (JAQing Off). These are an online form of the concealed objection technique listed above.

Sea-lioning

A sea-lion persistently asks for evidence or repeats questions while appearing to be sincere and civil. Every question is, however, in bad faith. They are one of the hardest kinds of trolls to deal with as they will draw you into what seems like a debate, but it goes on and on … and on … until you are completely flustered. The best response is to say, 'We don't seem to be getting anywhere here – next question please.' Do not, under any circumstances, invite the person to talk to you afterwards in an effort to get them to shut up. They will jump at the chance to monopolise your attention and getting rid of them will be even harder.

Chaos trolling

The chaos troll just wants to disrupt whatever social setting they are in. These people will often introduce side topics or irrelevant information that is designed to confuse and distract you. Chaos trolling can be carried out by bots, accounts which have automated algorithms or so-called 'troll farms' feeding the internet with vicious content. You can often spot a bot by weird biographies or very small follower counts – or by the same content from two or more people. Block and report the bots as quickly as possible – social media companies have automated ways of shutting them down.

Making a complaint

You can complain about trolling. If the trolling is coming from a member of another university, you can approach their university management directly and ask for a review. If it's a senior public figure or politician pressuring you, it's a good idea to approach your university media office and HR for help. While there's no doubt some universities will have a terrible culture of support, many are fantastic and know exactly what to do in these circumstances. Don't suffer in silence!

Notes

1   Jim R. Macnamara and Brenda Venton, *How to give winning presentations: A practical handbook for speakers to deliver effective presentations*, Sydney: Archipelago Press, 1990, pp. 123–9.

2 Erin E. Buckels, Paul D. Trapnell and Delroy L. Paulhus, 'Trolls just want to have fun', *Personality and Individual Differences* 67 (2014): 97–102, http://doi.org/10.1016/j.paid.2014.01.016.

3 Ginger Gorman, *Troll hunting: Inside the disturbing world of online hate*, Melbourne: Hardie Grant, 2019.

4 9 Reply Guys (@9ReplyGuys), Twitter post, 22 September 2018, 7:20 am, https://twitter.com/9replyguys/status/1043248639869681664.

Appendix 3: Making good-looking slides, graphs and visual aids

When you are presenting with visual aids of any sort, you are essentially communicating in two different but simultaneous formats. So, it is very important, particularly if you don't want your audience slinking off towards the exits in droves, that you don't convey the same information in both formats. Quite simply, if what you say and what we can see on the screen are the same, then one of those delivery formats is redundant. And please, whatever you do, don't go for the trifecta and also distribute printouts of your slides before your talk. That way lies Death by PowerPoint.

Do you really need visuals?

It's very easy to fall into the trap of making assumptions like 'I am giving a talk, therefore I'd better prepare some slides'. Instead, ask yourself: 'Do I really need to use slides?' And, even if the answer is 'yes', at least you have made a decision rather than just falling into lazy habits. The other question you probably should ask is 'Does the venue have a projector and screen set-up?' While fairly rare, it's still possible to turn up as a guest speaker to a conference or event with a USB stick crammed full of slides only to find they've moved the presentation to a rooftop bar at lunchtime with a stunning view of the city

DOI: 10.4324/9781003197713-23

behind you, but not a projector screen in sight. Been there, done that – not fun!

Images that illustrate

Let's assume the technology is there and you have decided to go with a slide show. Quite simply, a good slide deck is an integral part of your talk and sits perfectly alongside, but never mirrors, your spoken presentation. Slides should support, add to or illustrate what you are saying; they create a mood, provide visual examples or highlight memorable parts of your talk. They also help the audience retain the ideas that you communicate to them verbally. A well-curated set of slides tells the world that you are a consummate professional, whereas a badly designed, mismatched collection of text-heavy slides from which you read verbatim to your long-suffering audience just screams rank amateur.

So if you're going to be any good at this, not only do you have to be specialist in your field, now you need to be a graphic artist too (no pressure). Don't panic: it's quite easy to become enough of a graphic artist to be able to design impressive-looking slides without much experience or expertise. At this point, we suggest you turn to our friend the internet. The number of sites out there where experts from the world of presentation design will generously share their ideas with you is quite astonishing.

Less is more

What constitutes good design can be a matter of personal taste, but one of the foundations of successful graphic design is the 'less is more' approach. Putting too much text or too many images on a slide makes it 'busy'. A lot of visual information is difficult for brains to process in addition to speech. So, even before you get to setting everything out, reality-check every element on the slide. Make sure the graphic is there for a reason and get rid of anything that is unnecessary. You should be aiming for 'clean, clear and easy to understand', and, if you're really good, 'understated and elegant'.

While it is OK for a slide to stay up for a considerable period of time – in the Three Minute Thesis competition, for example, your slide is up there for three whole minutes – bear in mind that any time taken to read and understand what is on your slide is also time that is not being used to listen to your words and focus on your ideas. Ideally, you should aim for slides that take 3 seconds, maybe 5 at an absolute maximum, to take in. Not a second longer. Simplicity is the key to this; here are a few pointers.

- Keep the text to an absolute minimum. In fact, text is probably best left to the speech you will give; spell out only a few key words or facts on your slides.
- Steer clear of images that require serious interpretation.
- Be very, very wary of charts that require the audience to follow arrows, read the contents of boxes or otherwise work out what is going on.

Text and speech do not work well together

One little understood but important insight from brain science is that we can only process speech or read text – not both. When scientists look at brains in a scanner while people are reading, they see areas light up that suggest people are 'hearing' the words. While you are reading this text, think about how

Basic rules for making a hard to read 'slideument':

- Start with font that is too small, or inappropriate for the *seriousness of the presentation*
- Squeeze the text right up against the heading and use the whole horizontal length of the slide because you have so much to say and so little space to cram it all in. If you can make some of the points really long this means you cram even more information in, at the expense of comprehension. But at least you know that you gave everyone ALL the information they need and therefore they won't attack your ideas!
- Make sure you have bullet points because they create extra 'noise' for the audience.
- Don't put spaces between the lines to give the audience breathing space, like this:

- 'Negative space' or areas where you have blank background allow the audience to focus on the key information, but in a slideument you want to fill every part of the slide with text.
- If you want to put numbers in a slideument, it's a good idea to write them in your sentences like so:
  $P(Y-X=m|Y>X)=\sum kP(Y-X=m,X=k|Y>X)=\sum kP(Y-X=m|X=k,Y>X)P(X=k|Y>X)=\sum kP(Y-k=m|Y>k)P(X=k|Y>X)$
- Then make sure you **bold out some bits** so that people have yet another focal point. Or maybe use some *italics* and <u>underlines</u> to create other points of emphasis.
- Why not give up the bottom portion of your slide to as many logos as you can? I know, I know - we put them there in case people take photos.
- Don't forget to leave a hanging last bullet point (so people aren't sure if you have just been sloppy or forgotten something and include some text super small)
-

Let's give over all this gutter space to stuff that is irrelevant to what is on the slide and is more eye-catching than the information on the slide

Australian National University

Figure A.1 The slideument.

you are experiencing the words. If you listen to yourself now, as you read, you'll realise the voice you are 'hearing' is yours (although when you read 'Hasta la vista, baby', you might hear the voice of The Terminator). Your audience literally can't read text on your slide and listen to you talk at the same time because we can't stop our brains generating inner speech as we read. While your brain can switch between two audio channels quite quickly, you will experience dropout of one or the other.

We're begging you: don't create 'slideuments': an uneasy hybrid of slide and document. We've included an example of a slideument in Figure A.1 for your amusement.

You can't avoid text, of course, but keep it to a minimum and give people a moment to read it before you start talking. Or let the slide 'speak' for itself: let the audience read while you say nothing.

Style guides

Not only is the style and content of each slide vitally important, but the look, feel and design of the presentation as a whole contributes to its overall impact. To ensure consistency, have a look at your presentation in the Slide Sorter view. You should be looking for a uniformity in the design across the whole presentation. Always using matching fonts is an obvious example (and not just the choice of font, but also the sizes used, and consistency in the use of italics, bold, etc.), but this also extends to never mixing different elements like clip art, photography, charts, maps and so on, particularly on a single slide. You'll just end up with a mess.

Consider creating a style guide for your presentations. A unified look sends a subtle visual message that is professional but also underpins whatever mood you want your talk to have. You can extend this principle to creating your own house style that continues across your website, your blog, your letterhead, your business cards ... everything! Branding is not just something for commercial giants; it's also a way of controlling and fully exploiting the impact that you have on any audience you encounter. You can use the default branding templates provided by your university, but most of these are dire and take up valuable space in the header or footer. You don't need more visual clutter and words that will trigger the audience to inner speech.

If you are using graphs and charts, make sure they obey whatever set of rules or style guide you've set for the whole of the presentation. So, if the bar chart you've exported from Excel is pre-formatted, only comes in lurid yellow and purple and is set in an unchangeable font, you might want to think about redrawing it from scratch. And, if you are borrowing pre-existing images you've scanned from a book, while it's OK to use the image (assuming you have copyright), if it comes with any explanatory text or a caption, cut or crop that out and reinsert it using the font you have chosen to use for the whole presentation. While this might sound a little bit of extra work, it is only a little bit of work and the professional-looking results you'll achieve are well worth the extra effort. And while you're at it – take a moment to consider our colour-blind friends. Even the humble Excel spreadsheet now has colour schemes that are legible for people who process colour in a different way, so there's really no excuse.

There are thousands and thousands of websites out there that will teach you about good design and good typography. They'll show you where order and symmetry work to show you are in control, and where asymmetry and a touch of chaos can be used to dramatic effect. They look at balance and imbalance and teach you about the hierarchy of design – how the different elements in your design will lead the eye in a natural and logical way from point A to point B which, if you want your audience to understand what you are trying to get across to them, is crucial. You'll learn about a colour palette – the simple but hugely effective idea that if you choose, say, three or four colours that go well together and use them throughout your presentation, it will have a cohesion and sense of uniformity. If you have an image that is central to your talk – you might be a visual arts historian lecturing on Rembrandt's *The Night Watch*, for example – you can use a tool called a 'palette picker' to find your three or four colours from within that image to give your presentation even greater visual cohesion.

So, just as you hope that your words of wisdom will have a profound effect on your audience, if your slides are to do their job well, they should also have a bit of a wow factor. And, if you need inspiration to achieve this, don't waste your time looking at other people's slides; instead, go to the sorts of places where visual communication is of paramount importance. Go to any large retailer and see how they get their message across to their customers. How does Starbucks communicate this month's specials? How does H&M tell you where the fitting room is? What signage does a bookstore use to attract your eye to the new releases? These people spend a lot of time and money getting this right. Learn from them.

And lastly, while this might sound more like a presentation skill, it still relates to the look and even the design: there is rarely any excuse for using a laser pointer. If the position of an object on your slides can't be described with a tiny scattering of words ('on the left', 'in blue at the top', 'in the red circle'), you should probably redesign the slide. There can't be many more distracting, off-putting visuals than a jittery red dot wandering all over the screen during a talk.

Appendix 4: IP and all that

Inger used to have to run classes on ethics and intellectual property (IP) early in her career: no one would come. She renamed her classes 'Tragic Research Mistakes' and suddenly couldn't keep up with demand. The lesson? It's hard to make this rulesy stuff interesting, but it's important.

It's best not to learn about IP through your rights being violated and stolen. We don't aim to be complete in this section – just to highlight a few key principles and encourage you to explore more.

Types of rights

In most jurisdictions, there are three types of rights available for authors and creators.

- **IP** refers to ideas that you 'own' which can be passed on or sold. It can take a number of forms and can be jointly held with others. You can only protect IP legally in some circumstances.
- **Copyright** is one way to protect your IP (the other two are patents and trademarks, which we won't talk about more here as they are not usually relevant in a presentation

DOI: 10.4324/9781003197713-24

context). Copyright is the right to print, publish, perform, film or record literary, artistic or musical material. You also have the right to sell this ability to reproduce the work to other parties. In most cases, copyright has a time limit and can expire, releasing the rights into the public domain.

- Having **moral rights** over a work means you must be recognised as an author or creator of a text, idea or thing. In theory, you automatically own the moral rights over anything you create, but it can get complicated, especially in jointly authored papers. Moral rights don't give you any other right except recognition, and it is common to hold the moral rights but not the copyright. For instance, most academic journals insist you sign over copyright so they can reproduce the text, but they cannot assign another person as the named author.

Rights and presenting in public

Here's a short list of need-to-know stuff in relation to IP and presenting in public. Most of it is about moral rights as it's the most confusing part. It's not an exhaustive list, so please seek individual advice in relation to your project.

- When you present ideas in public you potentially create moral rights, but unless those moral rights are captured in some way, it can be hard to defend them. This is one of the reasons we have conference proceedings so people can be recognised as the inventor of an idea. A conversation where you express an idea does not give you automatic moral rights to that idea.
- If you don't record the idea in some way (say, by writing it down or in text form through a conference proceeding), you cannot stop other people reproducing the idea in text

form and claiming moral rights. In fact, this is one of the things that universities get the most complaints about from researchers. Often there is no way to defend moral rights, resulting in hurt feelings and anger.

- Moral rights are protected in academia through the convention of referencing. But it's just that – a convention. Not everyone abides by the conventions. If you want to protect your ideas before you present them in public, the easiest way is to put them in writing by publishing them in a journal, a book or conference proceedings.

- Does this mean you should never talk about ideas until you have them in writing? Of course not! But recognise the risks. If you want to protect an idea that is valuable to you, be very careful about how you talk about it and with whom you talk to.

- One way to have conversations and protect your ideas at the same time is to draft a non-disclosure agreement (NDA). Universities usually have an office that can help you do this if it's necessary. Usually, a university will only offer you this service if you are in the process of commercialising an idea and real money is at stake. It's considered very heavy-handed in most cases to draft an NDA before an idea is discussed in academia, but the rules may vary outside. If you are presenting research done in collaboration with a for-profit company, you will need to be particularly careful how you talk about the work in public.

- Some kind and generous people make their work open access, giving people the right to use it for certain purposes. When a work is released as open access, you do not have to seek permission or pay a fee, but you may have some restrictions placed on what you can do. For instance, there is a 'creative commons' licensing system, which can be used to make it clear to others how you wish to be acknowledged in any reproduction of the work – and whether they are allowed to profit from your work.

- It is good practice to assume an image or text is in copyright unless there is a clear licence for use included with the material. This means you have to seek permission to include copyrighted images in a book or thesis, but not necessarily a quote from a text. There is a provision in most jurisdictions called 'fair use' that enables you to use parts of someone else's work without permission for the purposes of commentary, criticism and parody. Presentations in public generally fall under this rubric but be careful – if the presentation is filmed and put online, those fair use terms may not apply.

- If you want to use someone else's words or images in a public presentation, you can do this under fair use provisions, but always make an effort to include the name of the copyright holder on the material you use, so that you are respecting their moral rights. If your slides are going to be included in a film or an online course or similar, you may not be able to claim fair use, so it's always worth checking where the presentation will be hosted.

- Copyright expires – or it can be 'orphaned': this is the situation where no one knows who owns the copyright anymore. With the invention of the internet, there is a lot more potential for images and text to travel separated from their creators and owners. Strictly, one should wait until the copyright has expired to use the work, but orphaned works may fall under fair use provisions if a 'diligent search' has been undertaken. Consult with your university as to what they consider a 'diligent search': usually there is a record-keeping process they will ask you to use as evidence.

Clear? Maybe not! If you are confused, seek help. There is usually a copyright officer in every institution who can provide expert assistance to staff and students.

Index

Note: **Bold** page numbers refer to tables and *italic* page numbers refer to figures.

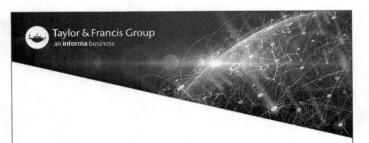